# ROCK THE TECH STAGE

## HOW THE BEST SPEAKERS IN TECH PRESENT IDEAS AND PITCH PRODUCTS

*Oscar Santolalla*

Apress®

*Rock the Tech Stage: How the Best Speakers in Tech Present Ideas and Pitch Products*

Oscar Santolalla
HELSINKI, Finland

ISBN-13 (pbk): 978-1-4842-6311-2  ISBN-13 (electronic): 978-1-4842-6312-9
https://doi.org/10.1007/978-1-4842-6312-9

## Copyright © 2020 by Oscar Santolalla

This work is subject to copyright. All rights are reserved by the Publisher, whether the whole or part of the material is concerned, specifically the rights of translation, reprinting, reuse of illustrations, recitation, broadcasting, reproduction on microfilms or in any other physical way, and transmission or information storage and retrieval, electronic adaptation, computer software, or by similar or dissimilar methodology now known or hereafter developed.

Trademarked names, logos, and images may appear in this book. Rather than use a trademark symbol with every occurrence of a trademarked name, logo, or image we use the names, logos, and images only in an editorial fashion and to the benefit of the trademark owner, with no intention of infringement of the trademark.

The use in this publication of trade names, trademarks, service marks, and similar terms, even if they are not identified as such, is not to be taken as an expression of opinion as to whether or not they are subject to proprietary rights.

While the advice and information in this book are believed to be true and accurate at the date of publication, neither the authors nor the editors nor the publisher can accept any legal responsibility for any errors or omissions that may be made. The publisher makes no warranty, express or implied, with respect to the material contained herein.

Managing Director, Apress Media LLC: Welmoed Spahr
Acquisitions Editor: Shiva Ramachandran
Development Editor: Liz Arcury
Coordinating Editor: Nancy Chen

Cover designed by eStudioCalamar

Distributed to the book trade worldwide by Springer Science+Business Media New York, 1 New York Plaza, New York, NY 100043. Phone 1-800-SPRINGER, fax (201) 348-4505, e-mail orders-ny@springer-sbm.com, or visit www.springeronline.com. Apress Media, LLC is a California LLC and the sole member (owner) is Springer Science + Business Media Finance Inc (SSBM Finance Inc). SSBM Finance Inc is a **Delaware** corporation.

For information on translations, please e-mail booktranslations@springernature.com; for reprint, paperback, or audio rights, please e-mail bookpermissions@springernature.com.

Apress titles may be purchased in bulk for academic, corporate, or promotional use. eBook versions and licenses are also available for most titles. For more information, reference our Print and eBook Bulk Sales web page at http://www.apress.com/bulk-sales.

Any source code or other supplementary material referenced by the author in this book is available to readers on GitHub via the book's product page, located at www.apress.com/9781484263112. For more detailed information, please visit http://www.apress.com/source-code.

Printed on acid-free paper

*Dedicated to you who came to the tech arena to build a better world*

# Contents

About the Author . . . . . . . . . . . . . . . . . . . . . . . . . . . . . . . . . . . . . . . . . . . . vii

Acknowledgments . . . . . . . . . . . . . . . . . . . . . . . . . . . . . . . . . . . . . . . . . . .ix

Introduction . . . . . . . . . . . . . . . . . . . . . . . . . . . . . . . . . . . . . . . . . . . . . . .xi

Chapter 1:   The Tech Stage . . . . . . . . . . . . . . . . . . . . . . . . . . . . . . . . .   1
Chapter 2:   Story . . . . . . . . . . . . . . . . . . . . . . . . . . . . . . . . . . . . . . . .   3
Chapter 3:   Killer Demos . . . . . . . . . . . . . . . . . . . . . . . . . . . . . . . . . .  11
Chapter 4:   Metaphor . . . . . . . . . . . . . . . . . . . . . . . . . . . . . . . . . . . .  23
Chapter 5:   Dataviz . . . . . . . . . . . . . . . . . . . . . . . . . . . . . . . . . . . . . .  33
Chapter 6:   Passion . . . . . . . . . . . . . . . . . . . . . . . . . . . . . . . . . . . . . .  51
Chapter 7:   Props . . . . . . . . . . . . . . . . . . . . . . . . . . . . . . . . . . . . . . .  61
Chapter 8:   Presentation Hacks . . . . . . . . . . . . . . . . . . . . . . . . . . . . .  67
Chapter 9:   Interaction . . . . . . . . . . . . . . . . . . . . . . . . . . . . . . . . . . .  77
Chapter 10:  Staging . . . . . . . . . . . . . . . . . . . . . . . . . . . . . . . . . . . . . .  83
Chapter 11:  Memory . . . . . . . . . . . . . . . . . . . . . . . . . . . . . . . . . . . . .  91
Chapter 12:  The Virtual Tech Stage . . . . . . . . . . . . . . . . . . . . . . . . . .  97
Chapter 13:  Get Started! . . . . . . . . . . . . . . . . . . . . . . . . . . . . . . . . . . 105
Appendix A:  Resources . . . . . . . . . . . . . . . . . . . . . . . . . . . . . . . . . . . 113
Index . . . . . . . . . . . . . . . . . . . . . . . . . . . . . . . . . . . . . . . . . . . . . . . . . .117

# About the Author

**Oscar Santolalla** is the author of *Create and Deliver a Killer Product Demo*. After a decade and a half in the technology arena, he embarked on a mission to help people in technology companies present better, inspire others, and sell more. Since 2014, Oscar has been hosting the public speaking podcast *Time to Shine*, for which he has interviewed more than 150 communication professionals. He works as a sales engineer at Ubisecure. Born and raised in Peru, Oscar lives in Helsinki, Finland.

# Acknowledgments

Writing a book is often said to be a solo exercise, but in reality, it is impossible without the inspiration and support from others. My special gratitude to these amazing people.

My family, my mother Lidia, my father Luis, and my brother Luis. My wife Mari for her support and the patience of living with a writer at home.

All the people I've interviewed for this book: Horace Dediu, Emily Edgeley, Elisa Heikura, Kevlin Henney, Mikko Hyppönen, Soledad Penadés, Richard Rodger, and Heather Wilde. You all are inspiring.

The Apress team for their support: Liz Arcury, Nancy Chen, Rita Fernando, and Shiva Ramachandran. You made me a better writer every day.

Anybody who has encouraged me to fulfill this new journey.

Thank you.

# Introduction

Out there, brilliant minds and passionate entrepreneurs are creating technology to solve big problems that our societies need today. But they all face the same challenge: how to spread their innovations, sell their products, and not be swallowed by the ruthless market?

The tech stage has become more vibrant than ever: thousands of conferences and meetups are organized around the world, spreading ideas, connecting professionals. But it's hard to stand out. "That was boring" are the words you hear through the clangor of a coffee room while people wait for the next round of presentations.

Your story can be different. You can succeed in spreading your new idea, product, or viewpoint and make the impact it deserves. There are millions out there who want to hear you, who want to hear brilliant talks, be inspired.

This book shows an unprecedented analysis of how the best speakers in the tech arena have reached the renown they had. You will read stories from Steve Jobs, Elon Musk, Panos Panay, and others who rocked the tech stage. Also, exclusive interviews with other less-known and also formidable masters of the tech stage.

Chapter 1 introduces how entrepreneurs, technology experts, and top executives have rocked the tech stage.

Chapters 2–11 unveil and discuss in depth the ten secrets to rock the tech stage: story, killer demos, metaphor, dataviz, passion, props, presentation hacks, interaction, staging, and memory.

Chapter 12 is dedicated to how to apply these principles in the virtual world.

Chapter 13 gives you strategies to get started.

The book also contains an appendix with a comprehensive list of resources that will help you find the right tool for the right occasion.

If you want to rock the tech stage, it all comes down to ten secrets that you can learn and put in practice. Are you ready for it?

**CHAPTER 1**

# The Tech Stage

You just got your badge and hung it on your neck. You are excited to attend the main conference in your expertise, the annual event of your industry. Your wishes are to learn the latest trends, to see very influential people with your own eyes, and maybe have the chance to ask them a question, shake hands, or have a coffee with them. As people start rushing to arrive, you can feel how people's spirits are up. The presentations start, you watch many, and in the last coffee break someone asks you, "How did you like the presentations?" Your first thought is, "Just OK."

With the growing number of conferences, there is a huge potential to educate, spread great ideas, share provocative thoughts, open up discussion, and ultimately make an impact. But, are we getting the best? Sometimes we do. When a speaker aces it, their videos or key phrases spread on social media like wildfire; those talks even reach mainstream and often become iconic. We should have more of those. Don't you agree?

## The Technology Arena Today

These are times in which the whole world is building technologies, innovations come from all continents, from both big and small companies. Today, the technology arena is more dynamic and innovative than ever; there are mobile applications, cloud services, artificial intelligence, clean technologies, blockchain, and so on. Also, there are more spaces to share knowledge and promote products. Both aspects make speaking about technology harder than ever: How can you speak about your product or company in a way that your audience not only gets what you say but gets inspired to become your raving followers?

© Oscar Santolalla 2020
O. Santolalla, *Rock the Tech Stage*, https://doi.org/10.1007/978-1-4842-6312-9_1

## Why You Should Speak in Conferences

I will split two types of speaking opportunities: for technical audiences and for wider audiences. Most speakers are active in only one of these domains, and they don't need to interact with the other. Either one you choose, your company needs you to get out there and talk about the technology, products, and what the company stands for.

Another strong reason is communities. Communities of professionals rely on conferences to share knowledge and keep members up to date with the latest progress across regions and continents. The communities are more international than ever.

## The Pains Techies Have

So if speaking in public is so important, why do very few professionals do it consistently and put in the required effort? Even though every person is different, the reality is that most techies enjoy programming, solving technical problems, or getting their hands dirty with machines more than speaking. Some of the biggest pains techies have are

1. Impostor syndrome
2. Can't put themselves in customers' shoes
3. The boss forced them to speak in a conference
4. Never had any public speaking or presentation training
5. Struggle to communicate well in a foreign language

## Ten Secrets

The next chapters of this book present ten secrets that have been used by speakers who put a dent in the industry, and whose products and innovations benefited from it. The ten secrets are story, killer demos, metaphor, dataviz, passion, props, presentation hacks, interaction, staging, and memory.

I wish that after reading this book, you get inspiration, feel equipped, and ready to rock the tech stage!

CHAPTER 2

# Story

> *Apple, I think, is run like a theater company.*
>
> —Jack Dorsey, co-founder and CEO of Twitter,
> in a lecture about storytelling[1]

At the beginning of the 1980s, the center of the attention was in the personal computer: the vision of one computer at every home was finally becoming real. There were several early innovators shaping up this new niche: Xerox, Commodore, and Apple Computer, among others. But also a behemoth wanted to jump into the wagon: IBM, the big corporation that already dominated the lucrative enterprise computer market. Coincidentally, one of the most ambitious products that Apple Computer had been being cooked for a while delayed so much that it shipped in the first days of 1984. Steve Jobs took advantage of the occasion to use dystopian George Orwell's novel *1984* and built his own hero story. Jobs' message was "IBM wants to dominate and become Big Brother. Macintosh is the only hope." Jobs used storytelling in a way very few made in history: allusion to a fictitious famous story. His exact words[2] in the product launch event were:

---

[1] https://ecorner.stanford.edu/videos/the-power-of-curiosity-and-inspiration-entire-talk/
[2] https://www.forbes.com/sites/gilpress/2018/01/21/apple-ibm-and-selling-artificial-intelligence-to-the-public/

> It is now 1984. It appears IBM wants it all. Apple is perceived to be the only hope to offer IBM a run for its money. Dealers initially welcoming IBM with open arms now fear an IBM dominated and controlled future. They are increasingly turning back to Apple as the only force that can ensure their future freedom. IBM wants it all and is aiming its guns on its last obstacle to industry control: Apple. Will Big Blue dominate the entire computer industry? The entire information age? Was George Orwell right about 1984?

The 1984 allusion was used in the remarkable Macintosh product launch, and also in a striking TV commercial "1984" directed by Ridley Scott (director of movies such as *Alien* and *Blade Runner*) and whose heroine character was performed by Anya Major. This story appealed to people who wanted to be different, the more creative ones, steering clear of the corporate business world represented by companies like IBM. Storytelling was a winning strategy in Macintosh success over its competitors.

Ironically, 36 years later a new video appears, and this time Apple is the villain of the story. On August 13, 2020, Epic Games, developer of the massively popular game *Fortnite*, released a video[3] that memed Apple's 1984 commercial claiming that they are the underdogs. The video ends with the quote "Epic Games has defied the App Store Monopoly. In retaliation, Apple is blocking *Fortnite* from a billion devices. Join the fight to stop 2020 from becoming '1984.'"

## Why You Should Tell Stories

These days, storytelling is widely mentioned in the media, almost becoming a buzzword, so I am not going to spend too much time in telling you why you should use them. From the speakers I have analyzed, I summarize all in three main reasons why you should consider telling stories:

1. Stories stick in people's minds.
2. Stories make abstract facts into more digestible to understand ideas.
3. Your audience wants to know you as a person. If they like you as a person, they will buy you or follow your cause.

---

[3]https://www.pscp.tv/w/1YpKkNqYZbmxj

## Role Play Before You Show the Boring Slide

In 2015, during his last Cisco Live appearance as Cisco CEO, John Chambers invited Jim Grubb to the stage to show some demos. For years Grubb had been Chief Demonstration Officer.

Using a CityPass mobile app with Cisco technology and services in the background, Jim Grubb did a few easy steps to electronically get John Chambers' Senior Pass. Once John got the CityPass from the mobile phone, the clerk desk said, "Fine. Then what I am supposed to do?" This insinuated how the mobile app, with the assistance of Cisco services, made things faster and easier for customers, no longer requiring them to visit a desk to get help.

It is an excellent example of how you can create an engaging real-life, relatable scenario while presenting the demo. Only after that, Grubb showed in the big screen a single slide that explained the architecture of the components involved to make this possible. In other words, story first, then "the boring slide."

Most presenters do exactly the opposite: they start with slides and end with slides, which makes their talks hard to stand out. Cisco's method intentionally avoided slides and put all the effort in crafting a story and making it relatable and enjoyable. People will forget that final slide, but they will remember the story.

## The Internet Is on Fire

On my podcast Time to Shine,[4] I have had conversations with lots of interesting public speakers, and during the very first months on air, I interviewed Mikko Hyppönen, a cybersecurity expert working as Chief Research Officer at F-Secure. When I asked him "what was your best ever opener?" or put it in a different way "what is the best way to start a presentation and instantly grab your audience's attention?" His first words were "stories work." Then he explained how he chose a real story of survival to open that excellent TEDx talk "The Internet Is on Fire (December 2014)."[5] The story tells of a young waiter called Walter Bailey who was the only person who took prompt action to try to save lives when a devastating fire was imminent at Beverly Hills Supper Club on the night of May 28, 1977. Bailey's determined action saved the lives of hundreds of people. As other members of the staff were slow to take action so he grabbed the mic in the middle of the band playing and said to everybody "there is a fire and you must evacuate the building now." Hyppönen used this as a metaphor for today's Internet, where everybody knew about nation-states' surveillance but very few people were taking action.

Stories are among the best ways to start a talk.

---

[4]https://www.timetoshinepodcast.com/
[5]https://youtu.be/QKe-aO44R7k

# When Stories Humanize Products

Jane Chen is the CEO and co-founder of Embrace Innovations. Often Chen starts her talks with a short story of a premature baby so tiny that can fit between an adult's hands, and she shows that baby's photo on the big screen. In that photo it looks like the baby is resting calmly, but in fact he is struggling to stay alive because he can't regulate his own body temperature. Then she explains that this baby is just one example out of millions of babies every year. With this story, Chen illustrates what Embrace Infant Warmers are: a substitute for a baby incubator used in rural and remote areas of the world. In addition to this opening story, she always tells a few more: her story of how the product started as a project during her MBA studies at Stanford and inspiring real stories of mothers whose babies were saved by the infant warmers.

What if instead she would start her talks with "our product is a cost-efficient neonatal incubator based on a pouch of phase-change material to stabilize body temperature for poor and remote areas"? You can guess: she would quickly lose her audience. Embrace Infant Warmers are a powerful example of a health tech product humanized with stories. Many teams across the globe, maybe even yours, are working hard to solve big problems humanity is facing, but ironically their communication style can make them lose the human touch and consequently lose opportunities for the product to become successful and make that big impact they are meant to.

### EXPERT INSIGHT: HEATHER WILDE

Heather Wilde is a professional who every day wears many hats. She is CTO of a few companies (ROCeteer, TWIP), angel investor, coach, and she delivers about 50 talks every year around the world. Shortly after she started speaking in conferences, the organizers reached out to her and said "we have a lot of developers, but they don't have any management skills, we need people like you to speak."

Wilde likes to tell stories and uses them in all of their talks. If not a personal story, Wilde recommends you should find an example or a case study. The audience should leave the room with actionable information. People relate better if there is something in their lives, so the case study makes them thinking "if that business did this, then my business should do that." Make them relate to their lives and businesses.

In her talk "Keep Yourself Alive: Stopping the Effects of Burnout" (2019),[6] one of her points was "You're preoccupied with work." To bring this idea into life, she told her story when working as one of very first Evernote employees. When people experience this symptom of imminent burnout, they talk about work all the time. When she was near to burnout, every other word out of her mouth was about Evernote, even though nobody cared about the product at that time. She wore Evernote T-shirts, socks, jacket, "I just lived Evernote. My husband and my sister-in-law worked at Evernote so my family was merged in." Work was interfering with her ability to recover. To recover you need to take time for yourself after work tasks stop. There needs to be a definite break, and that doesn't happen if you are preoccupied with work.

## The First Ever Tweet

Jack Dorsey, CEO of Twitter and Square, is a masterful storyteller. During the talk "The Power of Curiosity and Inspiration" (2011) at Stanford eCorner, he showed the most of his arsenal. Dorsey talked about his inspiration for creating Twitter and Square, and beyond that, this is a brilliant lecture on storytelling with plenty of inspiration for anybody building products. I strongly recommend you to watch it[7] or listen to it.

He started the lecture with a story of how his parents met, the time in which his father co-owned a small pizzeria business in St. Louis. Since his childhood, Dorsey had a fascination with city life and a particular obsession with maps, which he collected in big numbers and put them on his bedroom walls. About his teenage he said: "I taught myself how to program because I wanted to learn how to draw a map on the screen. And then, I accomplished that."

How was the first ever tweet? Years before Twitter existed, Dorsey had been prototyping a predecessor of this application and using a BlackBerry using its email capability. So he went out to Golden Gate Park and to the Bison Paddock there. "We do have live bison in San Francisco, if you haven't seen it. They're awesome. And I typed out an email that said, 'I'm at Golden Gate Park watching the bison.' It went out to my service and was broadcast out to all these people. I immediately recognized two things. First, no one cared what I was doing. Second, no one else had a BlackBerry. So, I was alone in my sharing and also receiving. So, I was getting no information back. Wrong time, good idea, put it on the shelf." Years later, when SMS was available at any mobile phone, Dorsey took that idea back from his shelf and coded what ultimately became Twitter.

---

[6]https://youtu.be/zS-QsLsQGsI
[7]http://ecorner.stanford.edu/videos/2635/The-Power-of-Curiosity-and-Inspiration-Entire-Talk

Toward the end of the lecture, Dorsey said "The data has been really important. But I think one of the biggest things that has helped me is learning how to become a better storyteller and the power of a story. And by this, I mean if you want to build a product and you want to build a product that is relevant to folks, you need to put yourself in their shoes and you need to write a story from their side."

He closed the lecture referring back to the starting story of his father. His father's pizzeria co-founder found Dorsey and contacted him via Twitter, from an account "Pie Pizzeria." They tweeted: "Hey, Jack. I think I bought your father's company. We're using Square to sell all of our pizzas." This example is a dream way to end your talk: unexpectedly circling back to the first story of your talk. Dorsey made it fun and touching.

Then in the Q&A, Dorsey told how he also gets inspired by companies, as one of his answers was particularly all about stories:

> "Apple, I think, is run like a theater company. It has a great sense of pacing. It has a great sense of story. It has a great sense of execution. It's all event-driven. It's all stage-driven, the stage being a billboard and the stage being a keynote or the stage being a product launch. All of it has a very, very cohesive end-to-end story."

## Show Who You Are

Soledad Penadés, a Creative browser crashologist, formerly at Mozilla is a developer and speaker. She likes to keep people entertained and have them follow the whole talk. Even if they might not understand the whole tech aspect, they should at least enjoy the story. In her talk "Make Websites, Not Apps (CSSConf.Asia 2016),"[8] she started introducing herself and she said that she was a Spaniard living in the United Kingdom. As English was not her mother tongue, she found it difficult to understand some common British idioms. When she hears expressions like "it's raining cats and dogs," her reaction is "what?" Right after she explained the idiom "going against the grain," which she used for the rest of the talk. Her point was that modern web development goes against the grain in many ways. In Penadés' case, she used storytelling also for telling about herself, her regular life, and creating a human connection with the audience. And that is very important: show your ethos, show who you are.

---

[8]https://youtu.be/nARgq17LmBM

# Now Become a Storyteller

This section gives you tactical advice on how you now can become a storyteller.

## Types of Stories You Can Use

If you have decided to use stories from now on or want to increase your use of stories, you need to find those stories. Some are already written, some you will have to create them first.

The main types of stories are

- *Personal stories.* A real story in which you are one of the main characters. An example is Heather Wilde's burnout story.

- *Real user story.* A real story in which the character has used your product or service. It gives your audience social proof, to show others that your product has already solved people's problems. An example is Jack Dorsey telling that his father's former pizza restaurant tweeted him to tell they were using Square.

- *Fictitious story.* You create your own fictitious story that depicts an imaginary character using your product and enjoying the benefits of it. This can be done as a role play story. An example is Jim Grubb and John Chambers during Cisco Live Keynote 2015.

- *Allusion to famous story.* Take a story from a known novel, movie, song and make an analogy to the real world. People have deep connection with pop culture, so you can take advantage of it. An example is Steve Jobs using "1984" for Macintosh launch.

- *Borrowed inspiring story.* A real story, not related to you or your product, that you can build an analogy with the point you want to make. An example is Beverly Hills Supper Club story used in Mikko Hyppönen's TEDx talk "The Internet Is on Fire."

## Best Practices for Storytelling

Telling stories can be unfruitful too, if done wrong. This summary of best practices will help you make your stories always effective.

1. *Make an inventory of your personal stories.* Use a notebook or some digital repository if you prefer (e.g., OneNote, Evernote), where you write stories about yourself. Make a collection and keep always adding more. Think of the past, for every work you had, every important project you participated or milestone in your professional life, find at least one story on each. Also think of moments in which a product or service made your life impossible, or exactly the opposite when you had great experiences. Jot down all stories, the right time to use them will arrive when you expect it the least.

2. *Practice reading your stories.* It takes time until a story sounds clear and impactful to an average audience. You will find the optimal way to tell a specific story when you've rewritten it and iterated it several times. Practice using pauses, changing your speaking speed, and even the tone of your voice. Read out loud. Personally, I find it useful to record and listen to it, and then rewrite again.

3. *Use stories outside talks too.* A powerful habit that will help you to become a better storyteller is using stories at all times, not only when giving talks. For instance, if you are going to write a blog article, start with a story. If you are going to answer a question in an interview, start with a story. If you are going to lead a meeting, start with a story. Make it a habit.

As you see, there are plenty of ways to use stories, plenty of places you can find stories. Personal stories are often the best, but combining with other people's and fictitious stories will make you stand out.

Next time you attend or watch a talk that sticks in your mind, look back and ask yourself why it caused such an impact on you. The most likely answer will be stories. You will discover many useful techniques by reading this book, but if you could leave these pages with one takeaway be stories. Now become a storyteller.

CHAPTER 3

# Killer Demos

> When you do demos, you have to surrender to the demo gods.
> 
> —Mikko Hyppönen, Chief Research Officer at F-Secure.
> Interview on Time to Shine podcast,[1] April 2015

On November 22, 2019, Elon Musk appeared on stage to introduce a new vehicle, the Tesla Cybertruck.[2] He paired it with the slogan "Better utility than a truck with more performance than a sports car." People who saw the event remember two things. First, they remember that the vehicle had an outlandish and unprecedented look, neither sporty nor luxury, and it felt as though it was from a dystopian science fiction movie. Second, they remember that the demo was an epic failure. Musk wanted to prove that the car's windows were unbreakable, so he invited Tesla designer Franz von Holzhausen to throw a 1 kg steel ball toward special armor glass.

So, what happened? The glass shattered. Perplexed by the outcome, Musk said, "Well, maybe that was a bit too hard. But it didn't go through." They tried again and, surprise, the window's glass shattered again. Musk had no choice but to laugh out of embarrassment and continue with the show. The news immediately spread not only in the tech world but also in the mainstream media worldwide. The demo gods were not with Tesla that day.

---

[1] https://www.timetoshinepodcast.com/mikko-hypponen-public-presentations-about-technical-topics/
[2] https://youtu.be/6Q3uaepRCl4

As you see, even a failed demo causes people to talk about you. Imagine the impact of you having a successful demo. I wish we could see demos onstage more frequently, but thank goodness there is a legion of speakers who dare to include a demo in their talks and presentations. Kudos to them. Demos bring products to life, if you want to rock the stage bring demos to your talks.

## Demos on the Tech Stage

Today, when people think about demos, they are mostly in the context of sales. You see "Request a demo" on almost every software company website today, especially SaaS or enterprise software companies. In *Create and Deliver a Killer Product Demo*,[3] I present a comprehensive list of situations for demos. Most demos take place behind closed doors, such as in a meeting with a potential customer. This book focuses on public demos instead.

These are the most frequent situations in which demos accompany talks: product launches, startup pitches, and API demos.

### Product Launches

These are the stellar acts of all product demos. As with the Tesla Cybertruck, product launches occur at big events, typically in front of large crowds. Especially from the 2000s and onward, they are designed for the video watcher as well, beyond the hundreds in the physical audience. This is a onetime event, which in extremely rare cases will be done twice. There is no second chance, so we have to do it right. Without doubt, Steve Jobs is who brought the magic of product launch demos to its peak. The biggest brands in computer software, consumer electronics, and the automotive industry do these types of demos every year.

### Startup Pitches

Across the world, there are startup organizations that arrange pitching competitions at least annually. It's a dream opportunity for passionate innovators who believe their new products can take a big leap, touch the sky, and win a juicy funding. As you might know, pitches are short presentations in which the teams have to relay the most relevant stories and facts to investors and other influencers in the ecosystem. Due to the short time of these acts,

---

[3]https://www.apress.com/gp/book/9781484239537

demos within pitches are rare. But if you can steal half a minute or less and include a demo, you can supercharge your pitch. Ironically, many events call themselves "demo day" but don't include demos. So if you participate in such an event, do justice to the event's name and bring a demo.

**What is a pitch?** In business, the term pitch is usually equivalent to elevator pitch. Here is a definition:[4]

Elevator pitch is a slang term used to describe a brief speech that outlines an idea for a product, service, or project. The name comes from the notion that the speech should be delivered in the short time period of an elevator ride, usually 20–60 seconds.

In the financial world, the speech refers to an entrepreneur's attempt to convince a venture capitalist that a business idea is worth investing in.

## API Demos

In developer conferences, the application programming interface (API) is a common topic that is spoken about. A bulk of the audience would be happy to see the latest APIs of both famous and lesser-known companies. Thus, what could be a better way to show the power of an API than with a live demo? If the presenter can code a few lines on the fly, display it on the big screen, and immediately show a result, that's proof that the API is powerful and easy. Doing this is called "live coding," and the one who presents typically is the API evangelist or developer advocate.

API demos have three elements that are worth mentioning:

1. *Your API must look easy.* Obvious, right? Your company might have an API with easy onboarding, usability, scalability, maintainability, security, and a great business model. However, none of that can be proved during your stage time. That's why your demo must, above all, emanate an air of simplicity. You want the audience to feel, *I can code this API right now and use this service.*

---

[4]"Elevator Pitch." Investopedia, www.investopedia.com/terms/e/elevatorpitch.asp. Accessed 21 July 2020.

2. *Live coding.* The most exciting moment in API demos is when the presenter is coding live. Those are minutes of suspense: Will the demo gods be in the room? What is this amazing result that the presenter has prepared for today's show? A combination of good practices when put together produce jaw-dropping results.

3. *Audience interaction.* Have you noticed that a developer is always behind a lectern or table while live coding? It's almost impossible to avoid that, as you have to be typing on your computer's keyboard. As a result, your interaction with your audience is limited. You have to find creative ways to enhance your audience interaction and break that almost inevitable barrier between you and them.

## EXPERT INSIGHT: RICHARD RODGER, CEO AT VOXGIG

Rodger is today an entrepreneur who has been a coder for years and has done live coding himself. He acknowledges that some people can do live coding so well that it is inspiring. However, some developers make the mistake of assuming, *Well, I can code, so I can do this as well.* Some common mistakes developers make when showing code are

- The code is displayed in too-small fonts. If you are showing code, you have to be really careful and make sure the audience can read the code.

- A lot of developers prefer dark mode, where their background is dark and the text is a lighter color. That is actually not the best when you are projecting, and it can be very hard for the audience to see the font.

- To make things worse, often the code editor shows colorized code. For instance, some code is highlighted in colors like red or blue, which is very hard to see against a black background.

A final piece of advice Rodger gives is that you have to be careful and use the least amount of code possible. The code is a tool, a great way for explaining a technical topic, but the code doesn't explain everything by itself. The meaning is built by the context you give.

# Demos That Rocked the Tech Stage

When I was writing *Create and Deliver a Killer Product Demo*, I had the pleasure of watching and analyzing dozens of product demos. A few of those demos had such an impact for their presenters, teams, and companies that I often called them "the product demos that made history." I will now present you a short list of such demos in their own class.

## The Mother of All Demos (1968)

Douglas Engelbart and his team presented a series of demos[5] showcasing innovative technologies oriented to augment the productivity of an intellectual worker, the result of years of research at the Augmentation Research Center (ARC) from Stanford University's Stanford Research Institute (SRI). Unlike most of the other examples you will hear in this book, this was not a commercial product demo, as the innovations presented took more than a decade to become mainstream products. And this is what makes it remarkable. I am not familiar with any other research demo session in computer history as remembered as this, and whose story was told in books such as Walter Isaacson's *The Innovators*.[6] Engelbart was the main presenter in the show, and the team unveiled many unseen technologies: hypertexts, text processor, collaborative real-time text editor, and the mouse, among others. On top of that—and what made the session more extraordinary—was the fact that they created a videoconference between the auditorium in San Francisco and the research center lab in Menlo Park. The demo session lasted 100 minutes, had almost no technical glitches, and ended with a standing ovation.

## Macintosh Launch (1984)

For this event,[7] Steve Jobs combined the idea of Apple's new product with the story behind George Orwell's dystopian novel *1984*. "Big Brother" is IBM, and the only hope is Apple. In the product launch, Jobs explained why this was a revolutionary product in the computer industry. He started the demo by taking a Macintosh from a bag, plugging it to the electricity, switching it on, and inserting a floppy disk he took from his pocket. Then the demo ran by

---

[5] https://youtu.be/yJDv-zdhzMY
[6] Isaacson, Walter. "The Innovators. How a Group of Hackers, Geniuses, and Geeks Created the Digital Revolution." Simon & Schuster (October 6, 2015).
[7] https://youtu.be/2B-XwPjn9YY

itself, showing a series of graphics ahead of any competitor's product and playing Vangelis' theme song from *Chariots of Fire* in the background. In the final section of the demo, the music stops and we hear Macintosh introducing itself with a humanoid voice. A perfect show ended with minutes of standing ovation and hurrahs.

## iPhone Launch (2007)

For many the iPhone launch[8] is the best public presentation ever in the tech industry, and for some even the best ever in the business world. Indeed, it was brilliantly orchestrated. The slogan was "Today Apple is going to reinvent the phone." Since Jobs began the talk introducing the iPhone as three revolutionary products in one, he divided the show in three parts, so there were three demos focused on different capabilities of the iPhone: an iPod with touch screen, a mobile phone, and an Internet communications device. One of the funniest moments of the demo appeared toward the end. Jobs was browsing the maps app, and he chose a nearby Starbucks café at random, retrieved its phone number, and with one click he rang the number. When the barista answered the call, Jobs said, "I'd like to order 4000 lattes to go, please," and then he quickly rectified himself saying, "No, just kidding. Wrong number. Goodbye!" That was the first known iPhone call.

## Minecraft on Microsoft HoloLens (2015)

The main reason this demo[9] grabbed my attention is that it has the perfect structure. Lydia Winters (Mojang) began telling the audience how Minecraft changed her life the way it did for millions of people, and she swiftly introduced Saxs Persson (Microsoft), who explained the technique that would be used to show augmented reality to the audience simultaneously. The demo was ready to start. Both started playing the game, and, as expected, the game was projected on the wall. Then, suddenly, Persson said, "Create World!" The "wow" moment happened: a holographic Minecraft world appeared on the empty table. The two presenters played a bit more, and then Winters closed with the words "From playing Minecraft on your wall to an entire world right on your table, Microsoft HoloLens gives the community a different way to play the worlds they already love."

---

[8] https://youtu.be/VKpaK67OU7s
[9] https://youtu.be/xgakdcEzVwg

## Other Demos Worth Watching

There are plenty of other successful demos to watch and learn from. The following is a list that I recommend, and I anticipate that you will enjoy it and learn great ideas:

1. iPod Launch (2001)[10]
2. Twilio's John Britton at the NY Tech Meetup (August 2010)[11]
3. Tesla vs. Audi Refueling Contest (2013)[12]
4. Athos 'Smart' Gym Clothes (2014)[13]
5. Tesla Powerwall Keynote (2015)[14]
6. Tesla Model X Launch (2015)[15]
7. Surface Book Reveal (2015)[16]
8. Surface Studio Launch (2016)[17]

## How to Give a Great Demo

Now that you have a sense of the magic that a demo can bring to your public appearances and talks, how can you give a great demo yourself? In this section, I will shed some light on the preparations you need, all summarized in three core points: creativity, structure, and practice.

---

[10] https://youtu.be/1vOXzcKqIPM
[11] https://youtu.be/-VuXIgp9S7o
[12] https://youtu.be/6_XEv2f_Uhw
[13] https://youtu.be/U5jAPKHFuSA
[14] https://youtu.be/OIgzzAMgnSU
[15] https://youtu.be/eWIt4Ze7r9Y
[16] https://youtu.be/OMTiD6AB4fw
[17] https://youtu.be/_wVt8djOGJU

## No Creativity, No Demo

In sales meetings, demos are a critical part of the process and should also be flexible. One day you might have planned a demo, but the best thing to do was to drop the demo and have a conversation with the customer instead. Or you can have a second or third demo across the sales process. But onstage is different; you appear once only, and you will not have a second chance. Onstage you need to entertain and make magic. No creativity, no demo.

The pinnacle of a demo is to create a "wow" moment, a few seconds that shows the benefit of your product and will stick in people's minds.

## Structure Your Demo

Behind every good talk, presentation, pitch, video, and commercial, there is a well-crafted structure. You need to structure your demo well, too. The main three phases are

1. *Before the demo.* A common mistake presenters make is start clicking through or showing the product before saying anything. Before the demo, there are two things you can do that can help you create the desired experience for your audience. First, ask someone to briefly introduce you, which gives you credibility as the presenter. Second, and most importantly, say a few words that give context about what you are going to show. You can tell a short story, technical details that will be used in the demo, define the specific use case you are going to present, or anything else that fits the best for the occasion. Be short and clear, and let the show begin.

2. *During the demo.* When you give the demo, the best way to keep your preparation process predictable and constantly improving is to write a script line by line. Doing a demo onstage is a performance, so treat it like one. Can you imagine an actor going onstage without rehearsing a defined script? Not really. Write a script and improve it after practice until it becomes perfect. The last element that can make the difference between a good demo and a memorable one is the "wow" moment. Spend time with your team and combine your creative minds until you craft a "wow" moment, and then perform it with clinical precision.

3. *After the demo.* The demo is over, you demonstrated the power of your product, you convinced your audience, and you heard some "wow"s from the crowd. A common mistake at this point is to simply say, "That was my demo, thank you." The first words that should come out of your mouth must reiterate what you have just demonstrated. The audience might have a different impression of what they saw, so your task is to choose the right words to *tell* them what they saw. Don't let the audience make their own conclusions. Finally, leave them with a call to action: download and install the app, pre-order the gadget, try the API, give us the funding we need, and so on.

## Practice, Practice, Practice

From all of the demos that you have seen, the ones that have stuck in your mind or made you buy the product share a commonality: the speaker or team practiced a lot until they made it right. "A lot" means hours and hours of practice. The result was zero glitches and the demo looked effortless. Do not let the effortless feel make you think that giving a demo is easy and you can just try twice and jump to the stage. Using computer terms, public speaking coach Caroline Goyder said[18] that practice creates a backup drive in your brain that happens when you've done enough rehearsal. So, she claims that if during a performance the pressure hits and you go blank, that backup drive (your memory) kicks in and you know you will be OK. For a visual and illustrative explanation, Goyder recommended the TED video "The science of stage fright (and how to overcome it)"[19] by Mikael Cho. It is three and a half minutes well worth of your time, which includes Steve Jobs' rehearsal habits.

---

[18]https://www.timetoshinepodcast.com/caroline-goyder-confidence-under-pressure/
[19]https://www.ted.com/talks/mikael_cho_the_science_of_stage_fright_and_how_to_overcome_it

## Embedding Your Demos in the Browser

Soledad Penadés is a speaker who had the vision of presenting everything in the browser. For showing demos, she thought that she could avoid switching between the presentation software and another window to show the demo, and then go back. She always cared a lot about the flow and she didn't want to lose any single person in the audience. Penadés didn't want anybody to think *How did she end up in that?* She made several iterations of how to best embed demos inside the slides so that she wouldn't have to even worry about where the mouse was, where the focus was. Her goal was making everything super seamless that nobody could tell that she had changed the slide. Her ultimate goal would be to forget the concept of a slide, to have a continuous flow.

Penadés demonstrated audio clips[20] that she created herself. Because she was working in Mozilla, she was trying to explain to the world how to use certain features of web browsers. She was fond of things that make noise or display pretty graphics on the screen. She was focused on talking about manipulating video and audio with the webcam software, which could create moving pictures on the screen and have interesting spooky effects.

Even though creating multimedia effects on a browser requires coding skills, in her talks Penadés didn't focus on explaining the algorithm being used. Instead, her intended message was *Look at the cool things we can do*. She went to the Smashing Conference,[21] at which there are not only coders in the audience but art directors, UI designers, and more. She expected those attendees to think that even though they didn't have the technical skills to try for themselves, they would suggest their art directors to try that novel artistic technique. Penadés wanted to open their eyes and make them embrace the possibilities of the things that we could make on the Web. That's why as a speaker you need things to be playful, exciting, engaging, and not to lose the flow of the presentation.

Indeed, I agree with Penadés that keeping the flow of your presentation is crucial for a successful demo. As said before, you don't have a second chance. In Chapter "Presentation Hacks," we will dive into how Penadés embedded everything she presented on the browser.

---

[20]https://soundcloud.com/supersole
[21]https://smashingconf.com/

# Key Takeaways

- Showing demos is a great way to rock the stage.
- There are three most frequent situations in which demos accompany talks: product launches, startup pitches, and API demos.
- Take some time to watch the best product demos available, which will give you ideas for your own. Some of the names behind several successful demos are Steve Jobs, Elon Musk, and Panos Panay. Search for their videos and get inspired.
- If you can remember three top pieces of advice for creating and delivering your own demos, they are *be creative*, *have a clear structure*, and *practice, practice, practice*.

# CHAPTER 4

# Metaphor

*Relate your product to something that is current and relevant and that everyone understands.[1]*

—Marc Benioff, founder and CEO of Salesforce

As we've seen before, introducing a new idea or concept is often a tough challenge. Sometimes an idea doesn't land on your audience even if you explain it twice or thrice.

So, what is that missing glue between a new idea and common understanding? Well, exactly what the word "glue" made in the question I just asked: visual language. You well know what glue is, you know that glue is used to bind or stick two elements together, but most importantly you have just created a visual image of "glue" on your mind. Maybe you imagined a school glue stick or a UHU tube?

The lesson is: for complex and novel concepts, ditch the literal explanations and instead use visual language. After all, our world is already surrounded by expressions like that, and successful speakers are using it to rock the tech stage.

---

[1] Benioff, Marc and Carlye Adler. *Behind the Cloud: The Untold Story of How Salesforce.com Went from Idea to Billion-Dollar Company—and Revolutionized an Industry.* Jossey-Bass, 2009.

© Oscar Santolalla 2020
O. Santolalla, *Rock the Tech Stage*, https://doi.org/10.1007/978-1-4842-6312-9_4

## What Is a Metaphor?

You have likely heard of metaphors before now. So, what are they, and when are we really using metaphors and not something else?

First of all, think of visual language: when was the last time that you heard words that immediately made you create visual images on your mind? Visual language is the raw material for metaphors. You need that so that your audience can paint a picture in their minds.

Strictly speaking, a metaphor throws literal meaning in the trash and replaces it with words that represent it visually. It's not about explaining an idea, nor about comparing it with something familiar, but instead about replacing it with visual imagery.

## Definition of Metaphor

A metaphor is a figure of speech in which a phrase or word replaces another to suggest likeness or analogy between them. Etymologically speaking, metaphor comes from the Greek word *metapherein* (meaning "to transfer").[2]

Now let us review an example. Barbara McAfee used the expression "listening with your skin" during a TEDx talk.[3] Here the metaphor is "with your skin" which in this context means "deeply." As you see, "with your skin" has replaced the literal expression.

Something to remember about this concept is that, in order to have a metaphor, you need to

- Use visual language
- Replace literal meaning

## Everyday Metaphors

We hear, read, and use metaphors all the time, often without noticing. Here are just a few examples:

1. "It is going to be **clear skies** from now on."
2. "Your voice is **music to my ears**."

---

[2]Merriam-Webster Dictionary, www.merriam-webster.com/dictionary/metaphor, Accessed 23 Jul. 2020.
[3]"How Oral Tradition Singing Helps Us Live & Work Better Together." Barbara McAfee. TEDxBend https://youtu.be/1rRQulQnaoQ

3. "We're in **uncharted territory** here," as used by Danish Prime Minister Mette Frederiksen, March 12, 2020, about COVID-19.
4. "The demagogue is always **cherry-picking** the rare stats that back up their ideas."
5. "We are still not **out of the woods**."
6. "The company had **a pebble in their shoes** until they deployed our software."
7. "He's **head and shoulders above** everyone in the industry."

And there are many everyday metaphors like these.

## Some Famous Metaphors

Besides day-to-day metaphors that are part of everybody's language, some well-known people have created their own metaphors, and here are a few examples:

1. "One hundred years later, the Negro lives on a **lonely island** of poverty in the midst of a **vast ocean** of material prosperity," Martin Luther King Jr. "I have a dream" speech.[4]
2. "Focus on the **forest** and forget the **trees**," said Warren Buffett.[5]
3. "**Illuminate**" is the title of a book by Nancy Duarte.[6] She created that metaphor and repeatedly used it to convey the message that leaders must enlighten the path where the employees, investors, and customers walk through. Leaders have to illuminate the path, become **torchbearers** (another metaphor).
4. "From Stettin in the Baltic to Trieste in the Adriatic, **an iron curtain** has descended across the Continent," by Winston Churchill.[7]

---

[4] https://www.americanrhetoric.com/speeches/mlkihaveadream.htm
[5] https://www.berkshirehathaway.com/letters/2018ltr.pdf
[6] https://www.duarte.com/illuminate/
[7] https://winstonchurchill.org/resources/speeches/1946-1963-elder-states-man/the-sinews-of-peace/

## Great Metaphors Used in Technology

During talks, product launches, interviews, and marketing material, the technology arena has experienced remarkable metaphors that are worth showing you.

Are you ready?

Here is a selection of effective metaphors:

1. The **cloud**. That's a common metaphor that is daily used to refer to services that are fully on Internet servers, instead of on premises. The metaphor contrasts what is on premises (on the ground level), with the cloud (up there).

2. **Data mining**. Another concept that has been used for a while, in which "mining" replaces the idea of extracting value out of large amounts of data.

3. A nifty story on Teradata video[8] revolves around data analysts looking for insight. The video starts with the words "Somewhere in the **Data Wasteland** ... A fearless group of analysts struggle to make sense of it all." The 2-minute story ends with the apparition of a prophet-looking person saying "If you don't have the answers, how good is a solution?" The message is that without a good solution (Teradata Vantage) the data analysts are surrounded by nothing but **data wasteland**.

4. Citrix's video "Why Design Matters to Me"[9] showed five guiding principles the company used. The principle "Inspire delight" was illustrated with the metaphor "Giving your users a great experience over and over is the best way to **ignite fireworks in their hearts**."

5. On the first days of salesforce.com, the business concept was so novel that it was introduced with metaphors. The one to explain AppExchange was: **The eBay of enterprise software**.[10]

---

[8]https://www.youtube.com/watch?v=FvSgENWIvTI
[9]https://www.youtube.com/watch?v=CJT340fooKA
[10]Benioff, Marc and Carlye Adler. Behind the Cloud: The Untold Story of How Salesforce.com Went from Idea to Billion-Dollar Company—and Revolutionized an Industry. Jossey-Bass, 2009.

6. EDS, a consultancy firm later absorbed by HP, created a video commercial **"Building airplanes in the sky."**[11] After showing a surreal footage of a plane that is at the same time being constructed and carrying passengers, the video shows the message "In a sense this is what we do. We build your digital business even while you're up and running."

7. On MacWorld 2007 Keynote, Steve Jobs revealed that Mac computers would switch their type of microprocessors. For that announcement he used the metaphor **"A huge, heart transplant to Intel microprocessors."**

8. The **"walled garden"** is a business metaphor used for many years to refer to commercial strategies pursued by dominant technology firms. An example is Apple, who aims to retain complete control over the software, services, and accessories used along with their proprietary devices.

9. **A cryptographic hash is a sieve**. Mikko Hyppönen had to explain "hash" to nontechnical audiences. He came up with the metaphor of a **sieve**. You can take a flour sieve and you put something through it. The amount of flour that goes through to sieve is the hash and in digital hashing you can regenerate the pile of flour from this hash. It's unique. A tiny amount of data represents the original full amount of data.

10. **Writing to the steel.** Panos Panay was asked by a CNBC reporter if Microsoft as a device manufacturer was working on making its own chipsets. Panay replied,[12] "In part of the Devices team we have a silicon group that goes down to the steel. I think when you make software you have to make it together with hardware, we call it **writing to the steel**. This is important and being able to create silicon that proliferates through the product and brings the right experience through the software to our customers."

---

[11] https://www.youtube.com/watch?v=Y7XW-mewUm8
[12] https://www.cnbc.com/video/2017/11/01/ai-is-bring-computing-to-life-microsoft-exec-says.html

11. **Technology that fades to the background.** Another metaphor that Panos Panay used in a blog post[13] he wrote in 2018. He described that people who work using Surface Studio to create and design things feel an immersive experience.

12. **Devices that sing.** In an interview,[14] Panos Panay talks about devices made by Microsoft partners that create mixed reality. In particular a headset, and referred to these as devices that sing.

13. **The Internet's immune system.** Cybersecurity expert Keren Elazari gave a TED talk[15] in 2014 in which he described why hackers are the immune system for the information age: "Sometimes they make us sick, but they also find those hidden threats in our world, and they make us fix it."

## Create Your Own Metaphors

I hope you are now convinced of the power of using metaphors. You can of course use known popular metaphors or someone else's metaphors, but you can take a step forward and create your own.

Not many speakers in the tech arena use metaphors, and from those even fewer of them create their own metaphors. A person worth mentioning is Salesforce CEO Marc Benioff, who explicitly recommends that people create their own metaphors, as written in his book *Behind the Cloud*.[16] He believes that metaphors are a powerful way to communicate a message, and that it is worth it to make your own. He also recommends testing a new metaphor before sharing it widely. Try them on your closer circle to ensure they work.

## Similes and Analogies

Metaphors have their close relatives—cousins, if you will—which also use visual language to express ideas: *similes* and *analogies*. Now it's time to analyze what the difference is between these figures of speech.

---

[13] https://blogs.windows.com/devices/2018/10/02/meet-surface-pro-6-surface-laptop-2-surface-studio-2-and-surface-headphones/
[14] https://youtu.be/nCR4CTg0neY?t=559
[15] https://www.ted.com/talks/keren_elazari_hackers_the_internet_s_immune_system
[16] Benioff, Marc and Carlye Adler. Behind the Cloud: The Untold Story of How Salesforce.com Went from Idea to Billion-Dollar Company—and Revolutionized an Industry. Jossey-Bass, 2009.

## Simile

A simile is a figure of speech that compares two separate things, which normally starts with the words like or as. Etymologically speaking, *simile* comes from the Latin word similis (meaning "similar, like").[17]

Some good examples are

"Defend your gross margin **like a junkyard rottweiler**" by James Watt on the book *Business for Punks: Start Your Business Revolution – the BrewDog Way*.[18]

"I've said it many times before about Kevin De Bruyne, his feet are **like paint brushes**..." by Martin Keown, former football player and sport commentator.

At the end of 2014, Dr. Alice Bunn, Director of Policy at UK Space Agency, described Rosetta's successful mission[19] of landing a probe put into a meteor as **"like trying to land a fly on a speeding bullet."**

"It's **like playing a game of Tetris**. When your successes disappear but your failures pile up" by Mikko Hyppönen, during Slush 2019[20] talking about the work of cybersecurity professionals.

"Now, software on mobile phones is **like baby software**." Steve Jobs during the iPhone launch in 2007.[21]

## Analogy

An analogy is a comparison of two ideas that are separate. It allows us to explain something based on parallels and similarities.

Often an analogy uses similes and metaphors.

### Examples

A common analogy in the sales industry is "We hired the wrong applicant for our sales team. **He's a farmer, and we need a hunter.**"

In the preceding example, "farmer" and "hunter" are metaphors that represent two different styles of salespeople.

---

[17]Merriam-Webster Dictionary, www.merriam-webster.com/dictionary/simile, Accessed 23 Jul. 2020.
[18]Watt, James. Business for Punks: Start Your Business Revolution – the BrewDog Way. Portfolio Penguin. 2015.
[19]https://civilservice.blog.gov.uk/2015/03/16/im-a-civil-servant-and-i-work-on-space-programmes/
[20]https://vimeo.com/374914179
[21]https://thenextweb.com/apple/2015/09/09/genius-annotated-with-genius/

In 2008, Intel had the challenge to explain "dual core" to the general consumer. So they created an analogy: "**since the microprocessor is like the brain of a computer, a dual-core chip was like having two brains in a laptop—one brain can handle one function while the other brain is doing something else.**"[22]

The preceding analogy used the simile "**like the brain of a computer**" and "**like having two brains in a laptop.**"

"**Cellphones leapfrogged the landlines and there wasn't a need to put landlines in a lot of countries or in remote locations,**" Elon Musk during Tesla Powerwall launch (2015).[23]

This analogy compares the challenge of installing telephones in remote areas with the vision of installing electricity to remote areas.

You can also convert similes into metaphors, by removing the word "like" and—as in metaphors—replacing literal meaning with visual language. The aftermath is shorter speech and shorter phrases. And as you might know, shorter phrases are usually more impactful.

## Why You Should Use Metaphors

Now you know what metaphors (and their cousins similes and analogies) are. Not convinced yet? Here is a summary of strong reasons why you should use metaphors:

- *Metaphors simplify complex concepts.* Depending on what you have to speak about, sooner or later you will have to introduce a novel or complex idea. When you find it hard to explain a difficult concept that your audience can't relate to at all yet, a metaphor could be the best tool you can use.

- *Metaphors will help you connect your new or complex concept with an idea that is already familiar to your audience.* Every audience has developed deep familiarity with movies, popular songs, sports, famous people, food, commonplace technologies, and so on. Your task is to build a bridge between that familiar idea and your new concept.

---

[22] https://www.forbes.com/sites/carminegallo/2017/05/21/a-trendy-silicon-valley-buzzword-offers-a-valuable-lesson-in-effective-communication/
[23] https://youtu.be/NvCIhn7_FXI

- *Metaphors use visual language that is easier to remember.* We're using, hearing, and reading metaphors every day. Visual language creates long-lasting memories, and this is where the power of metaphor comes in.

## Best Practices

Finally, when you have decided to use metaphors as part of your speaker toolkit, the following practices will make your work easier and more impactful:

- Metaphors are effective when connecting two fields that are very distant, but your audience is familiar to one of them. For instance, science fiction, automobiles, computer games, board games, escape rooms, and computer hardware are some common fields that techies are fond of. Find the right fields or interests based on the demographics of your specific audience.

- Pay attention to cultural and geographical connotations. We humans share a lot but in every country and region there are habits, famous people, products, and laws that everybody knows but can be unknown to the rest of the world. Thus, a really good metaphor can work wonders in one country and be useless elsewhere. For instance, neuroscience researcher Wendy Suzuki said in her TED talk[24] at TEDWomen 2017 that **"Exercise is a supercharged 401(k) for your brain."** That was a well-crafted metaphor, but it has zero meaning for most people outside the United States. Great for one country, cryptic for all the others.

- Every time you hear or read a striking metaphor, write it down. Keep a record of them to create your metaphors file, and you could include similes and analogies, too. That will help you to find the right metaphor at the right time and will serve as inspiration to create your own.

- Want an unusual way to find metaphors? Read poetry. Communication trainer Ira Virtanen told me in an interview[25] "reading poetry gives you a ton of unusual, fresh, accurate, surprising metaphors and imagery. In sum, you can happily bid farewell to clichés."

---

[24] https://www.ted.com/talks/wendy_suzuki_the_brain_changing_benefits_of_exercise
[25] https://www.timetoshinepodcast.com/ira-virtanen-power-poetry-reading-public-speakers/

## Key Takeaways

- Metaphors are one of the most powerful figures of speech. The key reason is because metaphors use visual language.
- We say, hear, and read metaphors daily. Many speakers in the tech arena use metaphors to communicate their ideas effectively.
- Similes and analogies are powerful figures of speech as well.
- If you want to stand out, create your own metaphors. Your effort will pay off.
- Make your voice music to your audience's ears!

# CHAPTER 5

# Dataviz

> *Most of us need to listen to the music to understand how beautiful it is. But often that's how we present statistics: we just show the notes, we don't play the music.[1]*
>
> —Hans Rosling, global health expert and data visionary

It's your product launch, and it is crucial that you prove with facts why your new product is superior to anything else in the market. Or you might be a Chief Information Officer (CIO) showing key performance indicators to the top leadership of your organization. Or as a startup founder, you need to show financial projections, key metrics, and timelines every time you pitch. In cases like these, you have no choice but to present data. Very often the unique message you want to share with the world is behind numbers, quantitative facts, data, and big data. All of these summed up are what we call data visualization, or "dataviz" in the industry.

Onstage a speaker can be either drowned by a sea of charts, curves and tables, or surf a wave of amazing data visualizations and insight. This chapter will show the importance of effective data visualizations (dataviz) in modern presentations so you'll become a dataviz wizard.

---

[1] https://www.presentationzen.com/presentationzen/2007/09/data-is-not-bor.html

# What Is "Data Visualization"?

In short, a data visualization is the visual, pictorial representation of data in a way that helps enhance the message.

# Not All Visualizations Are Good for Presentations

If you have been working with business intelligence, analytics, financial reports, simply took an Excel course, or studied information visualization at school, you know that there is a plethora of data visualization types. So which ones would you choose as a supporting element for your presentation?

First of all, bear in mind that what is designed to be read will not necessarily be effective in a presentation. When you read a report either printed or on your screen, it normally comes along with well-written explanatory text. Also, you have enough time to jump between the text and the dataviz until you understand the information. However, when dataviz is introduced into a talk, the speaker will switch your attention to the screen for the minimum necessary time and then will continue with her speech. In other words, the insight of a dataviz must be captured by the audience very quickly, the same as though the speaker shows you a striking photo. As there is no time to overthink and analyze the dataviz, we can infer that the most complex types of visualization will be unsuitable for the stage. All in all, the range of choice narrows down to the basic types. And that's good news for most of us who aren't data visualization gurus.

## The Three Basic Charts

Since we should choose basic types of visualizations, let us bring a refresher of the three most common types of charts: pie charts, line charts, and column charts.

*Pie chart.* In this chart, a circle represents a numerical value (the total) and is split in sectors, as slices in a pie. Each sector represents a portion of the total, such as a product's market penetration in a country. The sum of all the sections makes 100% or the total. Figure 5-1 shows an example of a pie chart.

Pie charts are good for comparing values or showing composition.

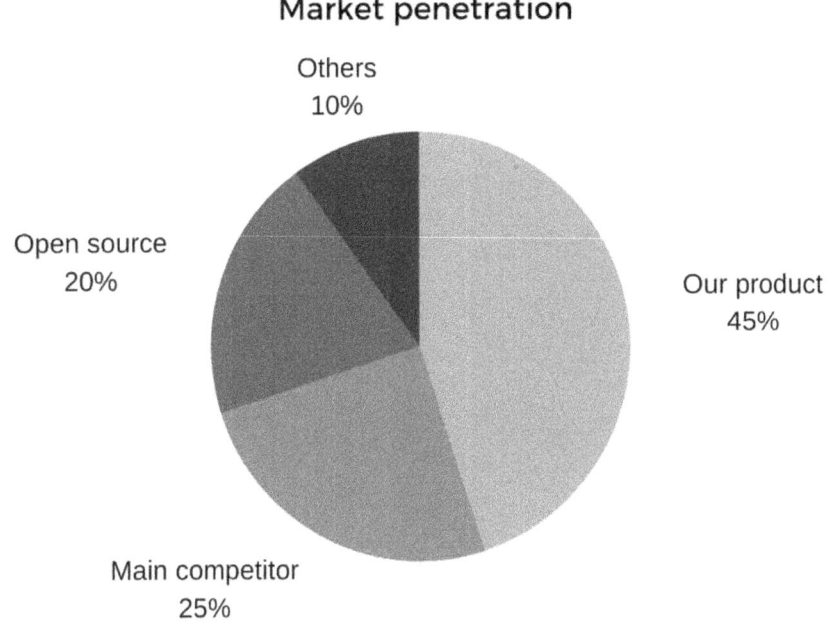

**Figure 5-1.** A pie chart

*Line chart.* In this chart, which is drawn on X-Y axes, the lines (typically horizontal) represent the evolution over time of a series of values or data points. Figure 5-2 shows an example of a line chart.

Line charts are good for comparing values, determining distribution, and analyzing trends.

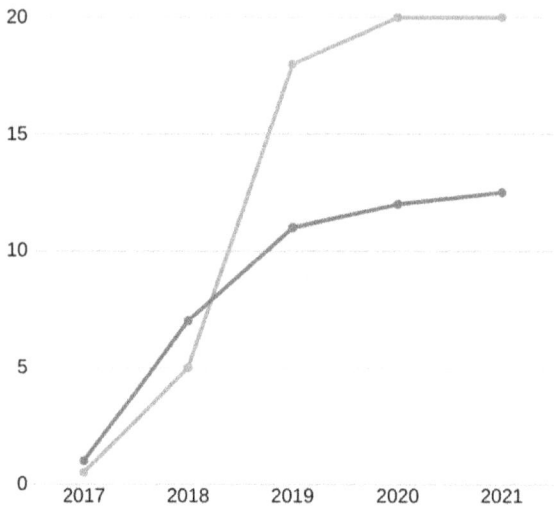

**Figure 5-2.** A line chart

Column chart. In this chart, which is drawn on X-Y axes, the columns represent different values that compare to each other. Alternatively, column charts can be used with the same purpose as line charts, to compare data sets over time. Figure 5-3 shows an example of a column chart.

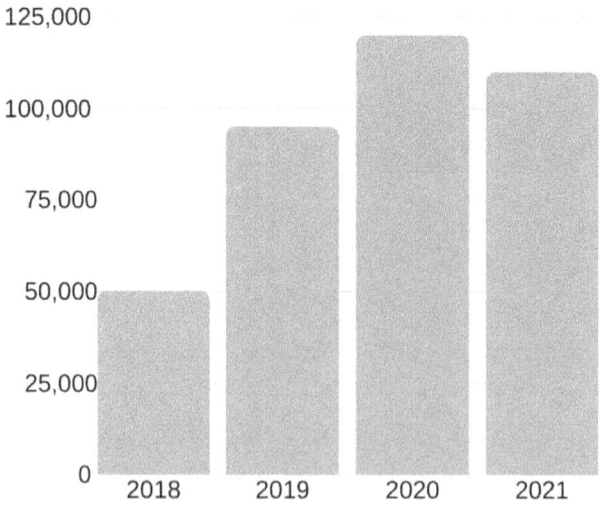

**Figure 5-3.** A column chart

There are many more types of charts, some of which are combinations or variations of the three: stacked column charts, bar graphs, area charts, combo charts, or doughnut charts. But for most of your talks, one of these three will suffice. Naturally, there are other ways of presenting data beyond charts, from simply using tables to cinematic presentations. Some of them will be explained later in this chapter.

## Common Mistakes in Presenting Data

These days, many speakers have already embraced the power of dataviz, have added it to their own presentation toolkits, and showed data in their magic acts at conferences. But not all data magicians achieved the desired spell in their audiences. What went wrong? Depending on the tool they used to extract, analyze, or display the data, many fall into a few common mistakes. Let's review the most common mistakes speakers make when presenting data.

### Not Knowing Your Point

Often a presenter has already some graphs in her hands, the result of putting a lot of data and getting a graph. Now the hesitation is: *Does this graph look good enough to present it?* However, the real problem is not aesthetics, the problem is not knowing the point to make out of that data. Make sure you know the point you want to make before deciding the type of chart and its aesthetics.

### Choosing the Wrong Type of Chart

A line chart, bar chart, stacked bar chart, column chart, pie chart, stacked column chart, scatterplot chart, bubble chart, waterfall chart, maps, tree maps, or a table. Which one should I use? There are online resources such as Interactive Chart Chooser[2] by Depict Data Studio that can help you choose the most suitable dataviz for showing your point. A deeper resource is Stephanie Evergreen's book *Effective Data Visualization*[3] which has an extensive chapter dedicated to choosing the right chart.

---

[2] https://depictdatastudio.com/charts/
[3] Stephanie D. H. Evergreen. Effective Data Visualization: The Right Chart for the Right Data 2nd Edition. SAGE Publications. 2019.

## Graphs That Are Too Busy

You have seen this. Remember that line chart with too many thick lines that overlap each other and, to make things worse, labels that are crammed too close together. All of us have attended presentations in which the speaker showed text-heavy slides while speaking to us (to make things worse, often reading the slides). The result: we had to choose between reading what was on the screen and paying attention to her words. Human brains can't do both things simultaneously. In a similar fashion, busy graphs force your audience to attempt to multitask while listening to you. Figure 5-4 shows an example of graphs that are to busy.

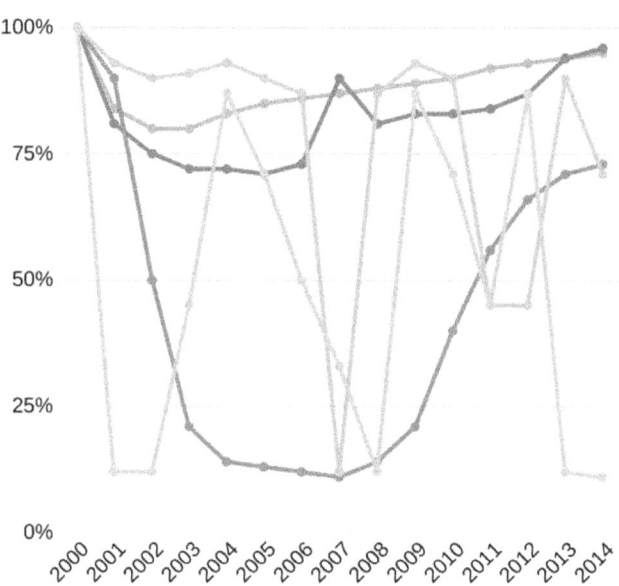

**Figure 5-4.** Example of graphs that are too busy

## Lack of Context

Sometimes the chart itself looks good and reveals information, but in what context is this information relevant? There is not enough information given to get a full picture. Aim to build a cohesive story, bring specificity for your target audience: year, season, industry, location or region, lifestyle, and so on. If there are too many elements to show in the dataviz itself, some can be part of the words you say instead.

## Titles Without Insight

In titles without insight, the words on top of the chart reflect exactly what you can see with the graph. The title might look obvious, but what is the analysis, insight, or call to action that the speaker wants to give to the audience? Later in this chapter, you will find the proper way to fix this mistake.

## A Blue Square on a Map of the United States

In order to generate solar energy, we need to fill large areas with solar panels, right? Actually, that's not precise. On May 2, 2015, during the announcement of Tesla Energy,[4] Elon Musk debunked that idea with facts. But instead of telling the numbers or even showing them on the screen, he used a simple yet effective visualization. His words were:

> "A lot of people are unclear on how much surface area is needed to generate enough power to completely get the United States off fossil fuels. Most people have no idea, they think that it must be some huge amount of area - like maybe you need these satellites in space - space solar power, if anyone should be in favor of space solar power it should be me - but this is completely unnecessary, because actually very little land is needed to get rid of all fossil fuel electricity generation in the United States. That blue square there is the land area that's needed to transition the United States to a zero-carbon-emission situation."

On the big screen besides him there was a clever visualization, which looked like Figure 5-5.

---

[4] https://youtu.be/OIgzzAMgnSU

## Chapter 5 | Dataviz

SURFACE AREA OF SOLAR PANELS REQUIRED TO POWER ENTIRE U.S.

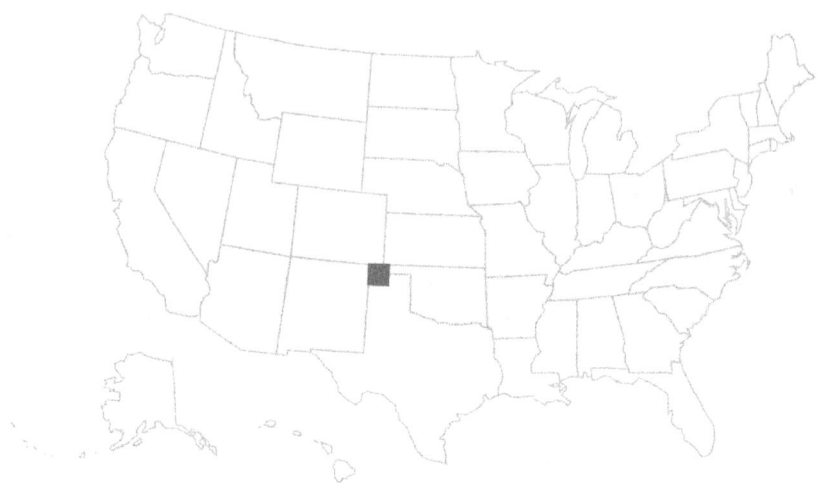

**Figure 5-5.** A blue square in the US map

Did Musk show any numbers? No. Any charts? Neither. The blue square within the map was enough to condense his point. Simple and effective, as all visualizations should be.

# Sometimes Dataviz Is the Perfect Way to Communicate an Idea

Horace Dediu is an industry analyst and mobility expert. During a big part of the 2000s, Horace Dediu worked as analyst for Nokia in its headquarters in Finland. He said that "Nokia's headquarters used to be called the PowerPoint Palace." The reason is that although the majority of people spoke Finnish, there was also a big and diverse international workforce (Dediu himself is Romanian-American).

Dediu felt that the way Nokia employees communicated more effectively was not through writing but through these very short bullet points and visualizations. It was partly as a need to simplify communication and not rely so much on long sentences. When he began doing PowerPoint documents, Dediu also realized that the slides which were most effective, which got most attention, which people stopped and asked the most questions about were graphs. They weren't the bullets, they weren't the diagrams, they weren't the clouds and the funny shapes. It was graphs. Why? Graphs usually contain a lot of data—the more the better. People in the meetings said, "Let's discuss where this comes from. It seems that the truth is here." Those kinds of comments on Dediu's dataviz already skewed his thinking that he needed to present data all the time to be credible.

## A Business School 101 Graph

It was the beginning of 2007. Both analysts and consumers had been hearing rumors of a new smartphone and were asking themselves: *Can Apple really launch a successful mobile phone? Does the company have the expertise to do it?*

In the introduction of the iPhone launch event, just 5 minutes into the presentation, Steve Jobs used a simple dataviz to show the problems with current smartphones and how Apple's new product was the solution that people were craving.

Jobs chose just two criteria among all possible ways to compare mobile phones: (1) ease of use and (2) an overall degree of being smart or not so smart. Then he drew a very basic comparison to illustrate his point and at the same time ridicule his competitors. Figure 5-6 shows such comparison.

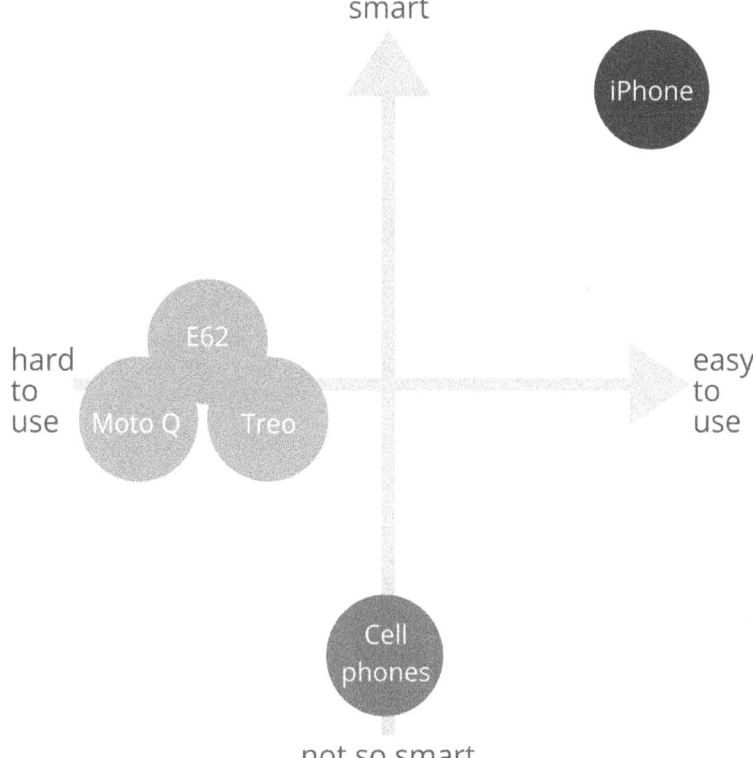

**Figure 5-6.** Comparing mobile phones in 2007

In this case, the key success factor was to narrow down the comparison to only two metrics, which is easy to manifest in a dataviz. Even though the chart was subjective and inflated iPhones, keeping it easy made this understandable and memorable. You well know that in real life when people compare phones to decide which one to buy, they have to read 10 to 20 specifications per device. Would that detailed comparison be useful to persuade buyers and media during a talk? Definitely not.

## The Single Biggest Reason Why Startups Succeed

Bill Gross is an entrepreneur and inventor based in California. When he was still attending high school, he started his first company Solar Devices with a very early vision of solar energy and successfully sold solar plans and kits. Later he founded and led several companies, including Picasa. In 1996, he founded Idealab, one of the longest running technology incubators. After decades of working with startups, he asked himself, "why do some startups succeed and others fail?" His curiosity made him collect data from hundreds of companies including his own, and he made comparisons based on five key factors:

- Idea
- Team
- Business model
- Funding
- Timing

The factor that stood out from the others truly surprised him. Gross presented his story and these enlightening results in a talk at TED2015.[5] See it for yourself in the following chart, "Figure 5-7. Top 5 Factors in Success Across More Than 200 Companies."

---

[5] https://www.youtube.com/watch?v=bNpx7gpSqbY

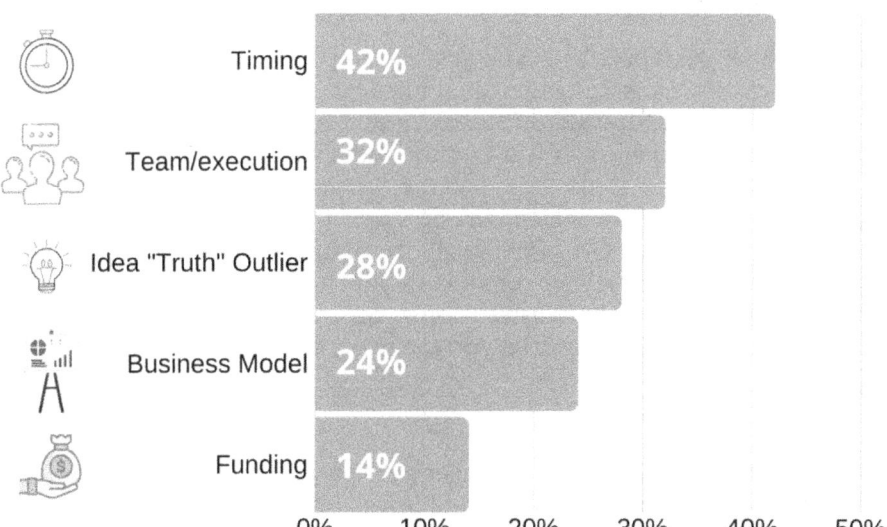

**Figure 5-7.** The single biggest reason why startups succeed

# A Data Storyteller Making Impact

Ben Wellington is a computer scientist, working as quantitative researcher at Two Sigma Investments. When he comes onstage, he introduces himself as a data storyteller. Wellington's own dataviz story started with his Tumblr blog "I Quant NY" in which he experimented using publicly available data of New York City and make visualizations and insight out of it. He combined two of his fields of interests: data science with urban planning. The result was informative studies of everyday life such as mapping the city per bicycle accidents' zones. Wellington's eureka moment—and the birth of the data storyteller—occurred when he noticed that it was his improv comedy background which helped him to make his writing much more compelling than other data science bloggers. That's how *I Quant NY* became popular.

In the talk "Making Data Mean More Through Storytelling" (TEDxBroadway, February 2015),[6] he described data storytelling in five steps:

(1) Connect with people's experiences

(2) Focus in one idea

(3) Keep it simple

---

[6]https://youtu.be/6xsvGYIxJok

(4) Explore the things you know the best

(5) Make an impact

Some of these steps have been said in some way or another in this book. The last one "Make an Impact" is worth giving extra attention. Wellington once sent an email to the city authorities saying that the reason why a place had a huge number of parking fines was because there was a hydrant that was hard to see. Weeks later he noticed that the authorities had taken action and marked the street as forbidden parking slot.[7] There he made an impact in society. Every time you find some insight based on analyzing data is an opportunity to make impact on your community: your customers, employees, other programmers coding with the same tool as you, and so on. Give a final thought and remember that by using data, you can make an impact.

## Cinematic Presentations

Horace Dediu became a popular speaker after he wrote a successful blog once he left Nokia. As he gained reputation of blogger and subject matter expert, he was invited to speak at conferences. When he started having talks, a couple of attendees approached and asked him to try a novel visualization app. It was the creators of Perspective app[8] which is available for iPad and iPhone.

Soon after using Perspective as his sole presentation tool, Dediu realized that what he was actually delivering were cinematic presentations. How his presentations compared to regular PowerPoint presentations was akin to comparing movies to photos.

Nowadays, Dediu organizes a workshop called Air Show. Air Show[9] is all about creating cinematic presentations, which is still a niche practice. Dediu is surprised that not many people are willing to do it themselves.

> "Out of 100 people who watched one of these presentations, I would say one or two come up and ask, 'How did you do that?' That's important. It's over 1% of people care to know when they've seen magic, 'How did you do that?' Then of those, I think 1% say, 'I want to do it.' That's 0.1% of people who want to do what I just did. Now, maybe we'll want to probably present, but to do that style of presentation because it is so unusual, it's just too somehow far for people to try to do it themselves."

---

[7] https://iquantny.tumblr.com/post/87573867759/success-how-nyc-open-data-and-reddit-saved-new
[8] http://perspective.pixxa.com/
[9] https://airshow.io/blog

On May 22, 2014, at Munich Kesselhaus, he presented a talk titled "Transformation of Business and Society through Technology."[10] The talk was part of the Futureday 2014 conference. Dediu started showing graphs of the life spans of consumer technologies in the United States during the 20th century. In chronological order, the technologies were: the stove, electricity, refrigerator, telephone, automobile, radio, television (TV), microwave, videocassette recorder (VCR), personal computer (PC), video game controller, cellphone, Internet, high-definition TV (HDTV), smartphone, and tablet. He showed how long each technology took until reaching 90% of adoption. After that, he introduced two more parameters: year of birth and life expectancy of people who lived in the century. With this, he showed how technology life spans overlay on human life spans. Comparing his own life span starting in 1968 with the respective newest technologies, he concluded that his family had always been early adopters. The life spans of technologies are getting faster and more unpredictable, such that the older generations and institutions will continue struggling to know what will happen in the coming years. Once the talk ended, the emcee asked for a final piece of advice for children, and Dediu said, "study the classics, because the liberal arts education are more important than ever, such as poetry because that is where the truth will lie."

## Lies, Damned Lies, and Statistics

There is a common saying, *Lies, damned lies, and statistics*. For decades and even centuries, people have used statistics and data to manipulate opinions. Politicians and advertisers do it all the time, but speakers across industries do it too. And data visualizations can definitely help with making a lie more credible and convincing. But hey, don't ever try to deceive techies. Techies have more critical thinking than a regular audience.

Elisa Heikura, a Finnish trainer and coach who has worked with hundreds of software developers, said:

> "When you're talking to a tech audience, they are very good at catching bullshit. They are also very keen on having the statistics and references and data and the studies. Those are the audiences that will raise their hand and ask, where did you get that? Where's the study? Who has studied? Do you have proof? Or where's the reference for the facts? So, I think it doesn't have to mean that you have to be an expert on everything. It doesn't have to mean that you know everything but be prepared to share where the

---

[10]http://www.asymco.com/2014/06/23/%E2%96%B6-horace-dediu-transformation-of-business-and-society-through-technology/

information is coming from. So no stealing of quotes, no stealing of data and stories without telling where the original source is because once you are labeled of being an unauthentic stealer, then the game is over for you as a tech corporate speaker."

## Best Practices to Present Data Effectively

All in all, we can synthesize the best practices to present data in a few concepts:

1. *Each chart has a purpose and makes a point.* Sometimes we have at our disposal a lot of data and a lot of chart options. Just imagine your team coming very proud after analyzing a million of data points with a powerful tool and bringing to your table plenty of data charts. It might feel intuitive and natural to show as many charts as possible so that we can prove our points. But take a step back and think, What is the message that I want to bring to the audience? What is the point I want to make? If a chart doesn't have a purpose for this particular talk, just don't show it.

2. *One message per chart.* To make sure your dataviz will transmit the message and insight you want, present only one message per chart. Stick to that principle. Remember the blue square in the US map? This good practice will be more crucial when the chart is complex.

3. *Tell a story.* The main problem with numbers is that often they are difficult to relate to. That's why it's crucial to make them as concrete as possible. Going a step further, a story will help you to illustrate your findings in a more emotional and sticky way. Go and rewind back, find a story to illustrate each insight. Imagine that you have to show "200% increase in social traffic during Q1" on a slide. First, begin with a story saying, "It all started when our colleague Laura posted a photo of our building completely covered by snow, and it went viral on Twitter." Then move on and explain the data. You should become a data storyteller too, as Ben Wellington did, and Horace Dediu with cinematic presentations.

4. *Use a McKinsey title.* This technique consists in writing the insight as the title of your chart.[11] The name comes from the management consulting firm McKinsey, which has such style of presenting data for decision making. For example, instead of "Referral Traffic," write on your slide's title "Twitter was our best referral channel in June" as you can see in Figure 5-8. As a speaker, use the title of the chart to persuade your audience about the conclusions you made from the data.

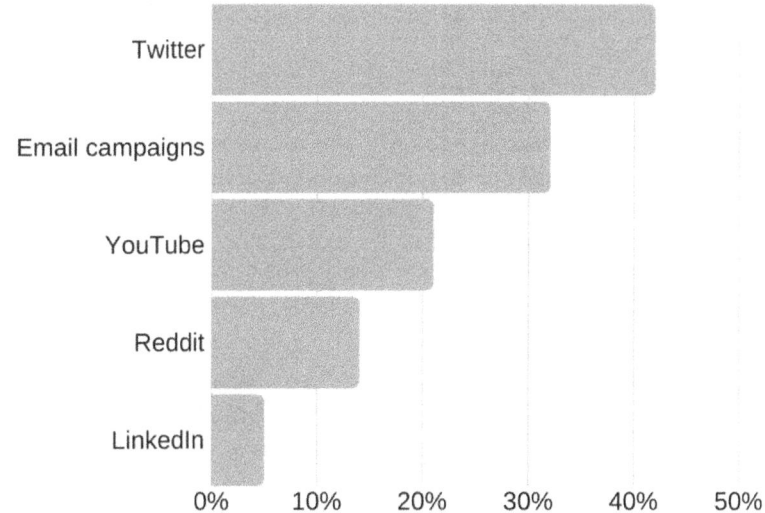

**Figure 5-8.** A chart with McKinsey title

---

[11]https://leapica.com/blog-bar-graph-google-sheets/

5. *Draw your own charts*. Most of us will create or generate our charts in tools such as Excel, R, Matlab, or something similar. Those are certainly not design tools though and lack the flexibility needed to present data. The obvious solution would be to use the default chart templates by PowerPoint or Keynote, right? Not so fast. Maybe for a school assignment they are acceptable, but not for serious business. Just forget about them. The best solution is to redraw your graphs yourself. This will be really beneficial for you. As redrawing can be an intensely manual work, this will force you to think twice before making an exact copy, as you would rather draw a simplified version. The resulting simplified graph will make your presentation much more effective. Therefore, the best is that you use a design tool and redraw your charts from scratch.

# Dataviz on Your Pitch

In Chapter "Demo," we discussed that a pitch is an opportunity with limited time constraints, and therefore it's important that every piece of information in a successful pitch is succinct and goes to the point. Let's also bear in mind that a pitch is persuasive by nature so it must convey credible arguments. So what would be more credible and convincing than a wisely selected piece of data? Here is where data visualization can help.

Most startup pitches include only a small number of charts, and each must have a striking effect on the buyer, investor, or decision maker. To accomplish this, you have to bring the right data in the easiest possible way to understand. Your audience must see the chart, read its McKinsey title, and get your point instantly. I recommend you review pitch decks used by successful startups[12] and look at the charts they used. You will observe the best practices to present data effectively that were outlined in this chapter.

Remember this. If tomorrow you had to give a pitch, what would be the only dataviz you would choose to show and what would be its title?

---

[12]https://piktochart.com/blog/startup-pitch-decks-what-you-can-learn/

Data visualization is a secret to rocking the tech stage that is not very widely used. But as you saw in the examples presented in this chapter from simplified country maps to cinematic presentations, a few speakers are telling stories effectively with dataviz.

## Key Takeaways

- Sometimes, presenting data is exactly the tool you need to illustrate or prove your point. That's why it's a good idea to learn the best practices in data visualization.
- Learn the basic charts first and, whenever possible, use them instead of more complex charts. Some dataviz are great for printed documents, but terrible for talks.
- Don't use dataviz to lie, and don't try to deceive techies.
- Storytelling is essential to presenting data. Always find a story behind the data.
- If you want to take a step forward and stand out of the crowd, try the not so well-known art of cinematic presentations.

## CHAPTER 6

# Passion

*When natural inclination develops into a passionate desire, one advances towards his goal in seven-league boots.[1]*

—Nikola Tesla

Often the reason why we pay attention to certain speakers, believe in their words, and follow their advice is simply because they speak with passion. Passion is contagious. And yes, we have seen passionate speakers in the tech arena. Even if you may feel that passion is an overused word, ignore that: passion is a great asset for rocking the tech stage.

If you don't show passion for your idea, product, company, community, or cause, then you can't expect others to follow your path. This chapter shows you that without passion, your message will never touch people and your idea will die.

---

[1] Tesla, Nikola and Ben Johnston. *My Inventions: The Autobiography of Nikola Tesla.* Experimenter Publishing Company. 1919.

## Talks Come from a Source of Passion

You might recall Soledad Penadés from an earlier chapter in this book about demos. She has spoken at dozens of small and large events, and her talks always have a creative touch. When I asked Penadés "what's your own motivation for creating new talks and go to speak?" she answered:

> "My motivation is that when I get very excited about something I want everyone to know about this thing. I guess it's coming from a source, from a place of passion about something. It can be anything because I like many things. Then the way I do things better, when I'm writing a talk, I can be fastidiously repetitive, and I will repeat the thing, and I will write it down, I will draw it, I will work lots on the skeleton of the talk. I will try it without slides, I will try to just tell the story and I will time it and see if that's going to fit. If it's not going to fit, I'm going to start cutting things out and making sure that it still makes sense."

As Penadés explains, finding a good new topic for a talk can be a long process and take a lot of time from a speaker. But the paths that start from a source of passion for something will lead to a talk that ignites fire in the audience.

## Developers, Developers, Developers

In the year 2000 at a Microsoft conference in front of a huge audience of software developers, Steve Ballmer (at that time Microsoft CEO) vigorously shouted the word "Developers"[2] 14 times in an act that the industry remembers well still today. Let's break up Ballmer's gestures during that episode. First, you can see Ballmer walking onstage from left to right, then from right to left for a longer walk, and then back again from left to right, so he was in continuous movement while speaking. In the video footage his blue shirt is completely covered in sweat, showing exuberant passion with his voice, and both clapping and fist punching to show his energy. So, we can say that he converged his words, body, and soul. Ballmer's example shows that if you put not only your words but your voice and your body into your presentation, you will energize your audience and they will remember you.

---

[2] https://www.youtube.com/watch?v=1VgVJpVx9bc

Besides "Developers, Developers, Developers," there is a second well-remembered video[3] of Ballmer in which after 30 seconds running, shouting, and jumping across the stage, he ends at the podium, stops for eight seconds, takes a good breath, and then shouts, "I have four words for you: I. Love. This. Company."

Ballmer created his unique style as über energetic speaker. Some people criticized him and countless memes of him were made, but his audience was excited and motivated with him. He will not be easily forgotten, that's for sure.

## Passion for Devices

Fast forward a decade and a half. Today, Microsoft's best presenter is Chief Product Officer Panos Panay. He has led the Surface devices portfolio since the early 2010s, and because of that he had the opportunity to be the visible face of Microsoft product launches. He has done a pretty great job. When he speaks, he can't hide his passion for the products the team he leads builds, nor can he hide his passion for detail and design. One of the best presentation tools in his arsenal is showing demos, which he enjoys and often co-presents with guests. Panay is also an effective storyteller who often talks about his life and his personal interests, and he finds ways to bind the stories he tells with his work of creating consumer devices.

When I see Panay in his finest moments, the only speaker that comes to my mind is Steve Jobs, and I wonder if the similarity is pure coincidence. In Panay's least brilliant moments, you can see him repeating expressions and words such as "incredible" and "critical" all the time. With passion, but too often. Regardless, Panay's passion onstage can't be ignored, and that is why many people admire him. They have made it evident in tweets:

@DamraBasil "My dream is to be passionate about what I'm doing just like how @panos_panay is." Twitter, 28 September 2019, 3:34 a.m., twitter.com/DamraBasil/status/1177743236791750656

@SmashDawg "Thanks @panos_panay -- passionate people and really transformative products make it easy to tell a compelling story!" Twitter, 17 April 2019, 8:12 p.m., twitter.com/SmashDawg/status/1118562786756517888

@NPDSteveBaker "And @panos_panay is on stage. Truly one of the best presenters in tech and a passionate advocate for @surface products and value proposition." Twitter, 2 October 2018, 11:13 p.m., twitter.com/NPDSteveBaker/status/1047218006613483521

---

[3] https://www.youtube.com/watch?v=f__n8084YAE

**Chapter 6 | Passion**

@ztlaidlaw "Goal for 2018: Be as passionate about something as @panos_panay is about the @surface line and the people that bring it to life. This man's tenacity and mission are infectious!" Twitter, 28 December 2017, 6:15 a.m., twitter.com/ztlaidlaw/status/946233128980533249

## Passion for Astronomy

Until recent years, we had heard of black holes only as an abstract, blurry concept. Nobody had seen a picture of a black hole except in science fiction movies.[4] But that changed in 2019, and the young computer scientist behind this breakthrough was Katie Bouman. Bouman had developed a passion for imaging since high school,[5] and during that time she learned about the Event Horizon Telescope project, which is an international effort consisting of a global network of radio telescopes. She had a leading role in the research efforts to publish the first picture of a black hole in April 2019.

Prior to that achievement, Bouman spoke at TEDxBeaconStreet in November 2016 and delivered the talk "How to Take a Picture of a Black Hole."[6] She talked about the scientific challenge of creating a picture of a black hole and explained the principles of the algorithm she developed for this purpose. Throughout the talk, you can see Bouman speaking with a fervent passion for astronomy, algorithms, and her work of research. She spoke in an energetic and fast tempo, constantly using her arms and hands to emphasize her words, using humor, and showing joyful facial expressions. She was always looking at the audience and she couldn't hide her enthusiasm. Thank goodness she did not.

If you watch Bouman offstage in interviews and such, you will perceive the same passion as well.

## Passion for Coaching Speakers in the Tech Arena

Emily Edgeley spent about over 10 years in cybersecurity roles in Melbourne, Australia, until she discovered a new calling and became a public speaking coach. After some bad experiences speaking in public, Edgeley decided to improve her skills. She watched many TED talks, got some coaching herself, and joined Toastmasters International. Toastmasters International is a nonprofit educational organization that teaches public speaking and leadership

---

[4]https://www.nytimes.com/2019/04/10/movies/black-hole-movies-streaming.html
[5]https://eu.jconline.com/story/news/2019/04/10/first-black-hole-picture-west-lafayette-grad-played-big-part/3426430002/
[6]https://www.youtube.com/watch?v=BIvezCVcsYs

skills through a worldwide network of clubs.[7] In her Toastmasters' experience, she became very active in running meetings, mentoring people, and building educational programs. She soon realized that she was getting so much more out of doing these things in her free time—more than she was in her paid work.

In the infosec field, professionals often get accreditations that need to be kept up, and every year you have to get certain credits. Edgeley got to a point where her accreditations were about to expire and she realized that soon she was going to have to quickly go through the course material, read some books, and do some webinars so she could keep her accreditation. So she thought to herself, *why am I rushing my accreditation?* At that point her heart was just not in it anymore.

Still, at that point, she never thought that she could make a career out of public speaking. She started to run storytelling workshops and posted some relevant content online, and it organically grew. People just started to seek her out. At her workplace she started to run events, and they would then get her to coach all the speakers. She started to get sent overseas to do storytelling workshops with the company's different campuses.

A pivotal point arrived in Edgeley's career where her organization went through a large restructuring. Several employees, including her, received three options: they could either re-apply for their current job along with about 5,000 other people, they could take a redundancy, or they could apply for another job within the organization. During that very specific time, she was in China with her boss doing storytelling sessions over there, and two very important things happened. First, a woman contacted Edgeley on LinkedIn and asked, *Can you coach me in storytelling? I'd like to pay you to be my coach.* Edgeley confessed that at time she didn't even know how to charge. That unexpected opportunity led to her first-ever paid coaching session. Second, when on a rooftop having drinks, Edgeley's boss asked her what was her decision about this restructure, Edgeley responded, *I don't know*, which was true at that moment. Her boss replied, *"Why don't you follow your passion?"* Her first reaction was to be taken aback. When she got back to her hotel room that night, she pondered, believing that he would have asked her to stay if he truly believed she was good at her job. But then, Edgeley realized that her boss was actually just trying to give her a little bit of good advice about following her true passion.

---

[7]https://www.toastmasters.org/about/all-about-toastmasters

Edgeley put in her resignation six months later. She started her new career in January 2019, without really knowing how she was going to make it work. She just knew that it was going to work because she loved helping people. Edgeley knows from her own experience how bad it feels when your fear of public speaking holds you back in many areas of your life and how liberating it can be when you come out the other side. She wanted to do her best to help other people to go through that journey.

Edgeley is now an established public speaking coach who works with individuals and conferences alike, such as Black Hat, BSides Melbourne, and the Australian Cyber Conference (AISA). She feels today that she has a nice mix of purposes: her passion for helping women in IT and security and her passion for helping people with public speaking. Edgeley wants to get more women on the speaking circuit.

## No Voice, No Passion

Have you ever seen a passionate speaker who speaks with a weak voice? Hardly ever. The reason is that speaking is not merely an intellectual activity. Yes, you'll spend a lot of time working with the ideas for your talk, looking for facts or the latest news items to back your points, writing and rewriting, creating slides and visualizations, finding the right photos, and more, but the ultimate product is *you* in front of the people. How you express the work you did will determine if you will be acclaimed or slammed.

When you're on the stage, the intellectual work is mostly done, and now your main job is to speak. The voice that you produce when you speak will make a tremendous impact on how your message comes across. People will perceive you as friendly, nervous, authoritative, clumsy, bored, funny, smart, or healthy. In most conferences and meetups, you want to be perceived as confident and knowledgeable but also likeable.

There is a lot that has been written and studied about the human voice, but to keep it short and simple I advise you to pay attention to the following:

1. *Speak loudly*. The best version of the sound of your voice is produced when you speak loudly. At most events, a microphone will amplify your voice, but it is best to learn to speak loudly without relying on the mic. When you rehearse your talk, speak loudly so that you can accurately predict how you will sound to your audience.
2. *Stay hydrated*. Especially during the 48 hours leading up to speaking, drink a lot of water. Plain still water is the best.

3. *Breathe from your nose.* Do you know the main reason why so many speakers have completely dry mouths after just 10 minutes of speaking? It's because speakers unconsciously breathe through their mouths. It's as simple as that.[8] Right now, you can try this: take a breath through your mouth. How does it feel? You might start coughing right away. Try breathing through your nose and you'll feel more natural.

4. *Melody.* One of the best ways to sound passionate and understood at the same time is to speak with melody. This means stressing the keywords in every phrase you say. You will not only be perceived as more lively, but you will also feel more enthused. Ultimately, people will understand you much better, especially if you have a noticeable accent or your speaking style is fast or monotone.

5. *Vocal exercises.* As singers do, vocal exercises are the best way to warm up your voice before a talk, and they keep your voice in good shape—creating the sound you want others listen to.

## EXPERT INSIGHT: CHRIS SCHOENWALD, PUBLIC SPEAKING COACH

Chris Schoenwald is a Canadian based in Japan who blogs and trains under his brand The Passion Fashioned Presenter. According to Schoenwald, in order to speak with passion, it is essential to step back, reflect, and ask yourself some poignant questions like: *What deeper motivations do you have as a person? And how could they be reflected in your presentation or talk?*[9]

- Other mental exercises include asking yourself questions like: *How would you like to be defined as professionally speaking ten years from now? How would you like to be remembered?*

- Also, study yourself when you are speaking about something you have passion for. Notice how you change when speaking about something you love. This is now your gold standard of speaking with passion.

---

[8]https://rogerlove.com/3-things-you-didnt-realize-are-hurting-your-voice/
[9]https://www.timetoshinepodcast.com/chris-schoenwald-speak-passion/

A final piece of advice from Schoenwald is that any time you veer off that path or notice your passion levels dropping, stop, reflect, and find ways to further wire your passions into your presentation objectives.

## How Much Passion Is Too Much?

If you recall Steve Ballmer's *Developers, Developers, Developers* act, you might think that his passion could be too much. *Do I need to jump and shout to be perceived passionate?* Certainly not. You probably have other examples in mind of speakers who sound passionate, but who you can't stand. It is not a good idea to imitate someone else's passionate style.

Be inspired by passionate speakers, but look for your own style. If you put in some effort and practice, you will discover that you enjoy the new passionate version of you. And your audience will enjoy it even more.

## Best Practices

After seeing the styles of passionate speakers, these are their best practices:

- Start by choosing speaking topics that you are passionate about. It's going to be very hard to speak with passion on topics that you don't care too much about. If you don't have the choice of picking the topic because of your job, find a connection between the topic and something you care about more, such as your hobbies, family, or another professional interest.

- Be ready to put in some extra energy onstage. Speaking onstage takes more energy than speaking in day-to-day environments such as chatting with colleagues in the breakroom. This is why you must remember to rest well the day before a presentation and stay hydrated.

- Express yourself using your whole body. Speaking isn't just an intellectual exercise. Remember: no voice, no passion.

- Find your own passionate style. Watch passionate speakers to get ideas, but avoid imitating them. Keep trying new ways of expressing yourself with passion until you find your style.

Are there passionate speakers in the tech arena? Yes, there are many, even though I wish there were more. Now you can be the next one!

# Key Takeaways

- Speaking with passion is essential for convincing others of your idea.
- Speak on topics you truly care about.
- There are many passionate speakers in the tech arena that we can watch and get inspiration from.
- Speaking is physical, not only intellectual. Once onstage, use your energy, your voice, and your whole body.

# CHAPTER 7

# Props

> *The seemingly impossible is possible.*[1]
> —Hans Rosling, global health expert and data visionary

When the time arrived for Steve Jobs to unveil the MacBook Air (2018), a laptop designed to be the thinnest ever, Apple had to find a special way to show its technological prowess off. At the start of the product launch event, Jobs compared with and ridiculed their competitor's products, but a couple of clever slides was not enough. How could he show this laptop to the audience in a way that impresses for its thinness and that people would remember this event through the coming years? The ultimate idea was brilliant: bring the laptop from inside a Manila envelope. You would normally put a couple of papers inside a Manila envelope, or you could badly cram a bunch of papers and documents, but who would think of putting a laptop inside? Nobody, because *obviously no laptop can fit inside an envelope*. The trick was a big success, it created a wow moment for the audience, and it became a video clip that will be known among the best presentations in history of both business and technology worlds.

---

[1] https://www.ted.com/talks/hans_rosling_new_insights_on_poverty/transcript

© Oscar Santolalla 2020
O. Santolalla, *Rock the Tech Stage*, https://doi.org/10.1007/978-1-4842-6312-9_7

For MacBook Air launch, the prop was the Manila envelope. If you are not familiar with the term "prop," you can think of it as an object used to enhance or create a desired effect. It comes from the performers' world, such as actors and magicians. The right prop in your presentation can make a huge positive impact and become memorable, so I encourage you to use them from time to time.

## Props in Pitching Competitions

If you are working in or if you are founder of an early stage startup, you will very likely have the opportunity to participate in pitching competitions. Pitching competitions give participants very short slots—typically two minutes—in which startups have to present their product, business idea, market need, growth plan, sales potential, and more to convince a jury of investors and startup connoisseurs. Often there is a monetary prize or the chance to meet one-on-one with established investors. In such a short time slot, there is little time for anything except the right words and the right slides. Even though some pitching competitions discourage or even ban the use of props, they are a powerful tool to consider. You could use a few seconds to show an object that will make your idea grounded and bring it to the present time.

A good example is CybelAngel, a cybersecurity startup and winner of the Slush 2016 pitching competition. The presenter was CybelAngel COO Evelyne Raby who appeared on the stage holding a thick bunch of papers. Soon after she said who they were and what CybelAngel does, she showed printouts of highly classified information that were found on the dark web. Raising a bunch of papers from her right hand, she said, "Here in my hands, I have the whole blueprints of the sensitive IT networks of a major bank. Here is the next product launch campaign of the largest luxury brand. And here are confidential technical drawings of unreleased airplane engines."[2] The fact that these documents were printed and just a few meters away from the audience gave a dramatic effect. In this case, the prop was just a bunch of printouts, as simple and inexpensive as that is.

A good question you can make yourself is: when to show the prop? There again, as a pitch is a short act, the earlier you show it the better. You can show the prop at the very start if it is used to present the problem (that was CybelAngel case). You can show it in the middle if it is used to present your product or other element of the solution. In this case, the prop can replace showing a full product demonstration whenever the latter is not feasible to do. You can also show the prop at the end of the pitch to reiterate or reinforce your idea.

---

[2]https://youtu.be/FCvXXDW5GjY

Finally, remember that the prop itself can represent the problem or the solution. A bunch of printouts was part of the problem, not the solution. Both choices can be highly effective. Sometimes the problem is difficult to explain but the solution is much easier to understand, and sometimes is vice versa. If you use a prop to present the solution, there is no better object to show than your product itself.

## An Overhead Projector

In the ending section of the TED talk "Fighting Viruses, Defending the Net (2011)," Mikko Hyppönen explained the concept of preparedness. He said, "Everything is being run by computers. Everything is reliant on these computers working. We have become very reliant on Internet, on basic things like electricity, obviously, on computers working. And this really is something which creates completely new problems for us. We must have some way of continuing to work even if computers fail."[3] A few seconds later, the stage lights went off and it got completely dark. He walked a couple of meters on that dark stage and switched on an overhead projector. To the audience's surprise he started placing acetate slides, containing in handwriting the key points and symbols to continue with his presentation. Indeed, the computer was not up and running anymore, but he used the overhead projector to finalize his talk.

This prop was rarer: an overhead projector plus four customized and colored slides.

Earlier in the same talk, Hyppönen had used another prop. He said, "So let me show you something. This here is Brain. This is a floppy disk -- five and a quarter-inch floppy disk infected by Brain.A. It's the first virus we ever found for PC computers." The prop was an old 5 1/4-inch floppy disk, which he later inserted in his computer and analyzed the virus. I am sure that many in the audience hadn't seen such a floppy disk before, and it had the effect of bringing us 20 years back in time to 1986. The interesting thing is that in order to do that, Hyppönen had to use (for his entire talk) a laptop old enough to have a slot for such disks. Most computers in 2011 didn't have floppy disk interfaces anymore.

## Inspiration from Other Fields

In this section, I will present a few examples from other fields that are worth reviewing and can be extrapolated to the tech arena.

---

[3] https://www.ted.com/talks/mikko_hypponen_fighting_viruses_defending_the_net/transcript

## Chapter 7 | Props

Hans Rosling was a speaker remarkable for his data visualizations and the use of props. Doctor by profession, he embarked on the mission of showing accurate facts and statistics that illustrate how the world is today and how much progress has been made. He knew that schools still teach a very outdated view of the world, which creates misconceptions and myths and prevents us from attacking today's most important problems. He became a famous TED speaker, and until his death in 2019 he delivered a total of ten TED and TEDx talks.

In TED2007, Hans Rosling delivered the talk "New Insights on Poverty." He presented eye-opening statistics to prove that the poorest countries in the world can achieve similar living standards as Singapore, USA and his country Sweden had today. Towards the end he repeated the phrase "The seemingly impossible is possible" and in order to prove it he ended the talk swallowing a steel sword.[4] Simply jaw-dropping.

In TEDWomen 2010, Rosling delivered the talk "The Magic Washing Machine."[5] He started re-creating the moment his parents finally saved enough money to buy a washing machine, and how his grandmother looked at the machine rotating mesmerized by this technological miracle. A washing machine was on the stage, he put some laundry in, and saw the machine rotating. Owning a machine is a sign of either wealth or poverty, and in the poorest countries the women spend many hours per week washing by hand. In some regions they even have to walk far and collect water before they can wash. At the end of the talk, he comes back to the washing machine, opens its door, and instead of taking the laundry washed, what he gets is books. His point was: now that women don't have to wash their families' laundry, they can read books, tell stories to their children, learn languages, and enjoy literature.

## "Oh, You Think Smoking Kills"

In his winning speech "The Power of Words," World Champion of Public Speaking 2015 Mohammed Qahtani started by putting a cigarette in his mouth, a lighter in his right hand, rolled the sparkling wheel, and looked like getting ready to light the cigarette. As the audience started making comments and sounds showing their surprise—some were even shocked (*Is he really going to smoke in front of us?*), he stopped, looked at the audience, and said: "What? Oh, you think smoking kills. Let me tell you something. Did you know that the amount of people dying from diabetes are three times as many people dying from smoking. Yet if I pulled a snicker bar nobody would say anything."[6] Obviously, he didn't light the cigarette, he only used it to cause shock in the audience and illustrate his point.

---

[4] https://www.ted.com/talks/hans_rosling_new_insights_on_poverty
[5] https://www.ted.com/talks/hans_rosling_the_magic_washing_machine
[6] https://youtu.be/Iqq1roF4C8s

Here the props used were two: a cigarette and a lighter.

## Finding the Right Prop

What is the right prop for you to use? The first thing to remember is: you do not always need a prop. Sometimes an object will be obvious, but normally it's hard to find one. The following is a description of some different ways a prop can help you:

*Make an idea concrete.* If your product or idea is too abstract and hard to imagine, a prop can ground it. An example is CybelAngel's printouts of classified information, or Hyppönen's overhead projector to illustrate preparedness.

*Stress a product's capability.* Sometimes a competitive advantage is categorical but still not very impressive to the eyes. A prop can complement your product to stress such outstanding capability. An example is Jobs' Manila envelope used to unveil MacBook Air.

*Grab your audience's attention.* The prop is used to grab the attention and make the audience feel the problem or think of an idea. An example is Qahtani's cigarette and lighter.

*Dramatize a statement.* Words are powerful but sometimes an action of bravery can multiply the effect of a statement. An example is Hans Rosling's sword swallowing.

## Best Practices for Using Props

Once you have defined the prop or props you are going to use, you must take some considerations to make sure they have the impact you want:

*One is often the best.* With exceptions, the best is to have only one prop. Having too many props can become a distraction. After all, you want to make one point (or two) on your talk, not a dozen.

*Practice every single movement.* The right performance takes practice. Rehearse many times until you cannot get it wrong. If you have to speak and show the prop at the same time, practice them separately until both are fluent, and then practice all together.

*Take a few seconds to show the prop.* This specifically applies to objects that you will show briefly, once only, and then you will move to a different point. Show the prop, wait a few seconds, and give your audience enough time to see it properly before moving to the next point. If you need to move it, do it slowly unless the speed is also part of the trick.

## Key Takeaways

- A prop is an object that you show to the audience to create a desired effect on them. The prop typically represents a problem or a solution.

- Props can help you in different ways: make an idea concrete, stress a product's capability, grab your audience's attention, or dramatize a statement.

- Props have made product launches, TED talks, pitches, and speeches memorable and successful.

- Once you have selected your props, some good practices for showing them are: one is often the best, practice every single movement, and take a few seconds to show the prop.

- Use props whenever you can. By not being a very common tool, you will stand out of the crowd.

CHAPTER 8

# Presentation Hacks

> *If you think presentations cannot enchant people, then you have never seen a really good one.*[1]
>
> —Guy Kawasaki, chief evangelist of Canva

Think for a moment on all the talks you have watched. Can you remember one without presentation slides? That's quite rare. What about you? When is the last time you gave a talk without slides?

Presentation slides are a ubiquitous tool many presenters use. This is why—if we're going to use them—let's do it the right way. This chapter gives you some basics and also explores in depth the presentation hacks from successful speakers in the tech arena.

---

[1]Kawasaki, Guy. *Enchantment. The Art of Changing Hearts, Minds, and Actions.* Penguin Publishing Group. 2011.

© Oscar Santolalla 2020
O. Santolalla, *Rock the Tech Stage*, https://doi.org/10.1007/978-1-4842-6312-9_8

## Do I Always Need Presentation Slides to Speak?

The quick answer is: no. But slides can be useful and effective tools if they are designed and presented well. This book will not debate if you should use presentation slides or not, but will give tactical advice for using them effectively. Let's focus on how slides can become a magic tool instead of a burden.

## Design Well and Present Well

Let's analyze the two main phases of using slides for your talks: *design* and *present*. Put in a different way: before the stage time and during the stage time.

### Design Your Presentation Slides

Here we will answer questions such as: *Should I use Keynote, PowerPoint, Prezi, or something else? Should I use bullet points, photos, quotes? Where do I start?*

1. *Start with pen and paper.* One of the biggest mistakes in creating slides is simply opening PowerPoint and starting to fill a blank slide. Doing that will limit your creative process. Instead, grab a pen and paper and put your ideas there. Make notes, draw sketches, scratch them, create a structure, and decide on your stories and examples. Only when you have the content organized in your notes, go to the computer or tablet and use the tool to capture your ideas onto slides.

2. *Build a storyboard.* A good practice that expands on the previous idea is organizing your talk as a storyboard. The concept of storyboards has been used for decades in creative disciplines such as movies, comics, TV series, and commercials. More recently, it has become commonplace in designing games and front ends for websites and apps. Storyboards consist of a series of panels or boxes, in which each contains one drawing and optionally some text, all as a sketch. So you can similarly draw sketches of every idea you have in mind, and once you organize them in a logical sequence the storyboard is done. Once the storyboard is ready, you can open the presentation software and create the slides. Any modern presentation software will allow you to capture your ideas once your storyboard is well-crafted.

3. *Use a presentation template.* Do you remember yourself creating several slides, one by one, trying to keep some style, and later when you decided to change that style you had no choice but manually editing every single slide? That manual, mundane work is unnecessary. Most presentation software tools have the concept of a template. Invest a bit of time and learn how to use templates. In PowerPoint, you can find the Slide Master feature for using and editing templates (see Figure 8-1). Use templates to ensure consistency on the style across your slides and to save valuable time. As a result, you can funnel that saved time into creativity.

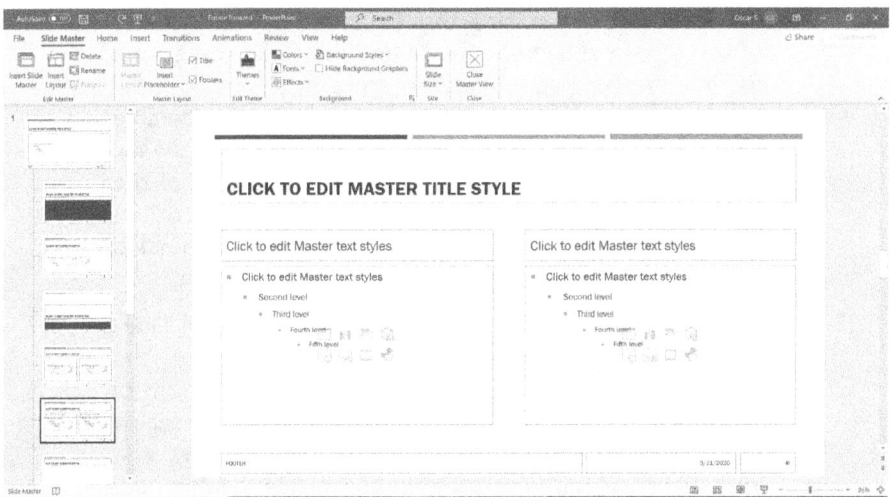

**Figure 8-1.** Slide Master. View of a template in PowerPoint

4. *Keep every slide simple.* Busy slides are the past and have been largely criticized with reason. Your goal should be: one picture per slide, one phrase per slide, one graph per slide.

5. *Beware of copyrights.* Today, many talks will be livestreamed or video-recorded to be published later. Make sure every image you use is copyright cleared. Use your own photos whenever possible as that will make your visuals more unique and will have a personal touch. If not, find copyright-free images in sites such as Unsplash,[2] Wikimedia Commons,[3] and others.

## Present Your Slides

Now that you have the presentation slides ready, you need to use them well.

1. *Find the best spot to stand.* Especially in small events oftentimes your speaking area is limited by the location of the screen and the table or podium. Take some time to find the best spot and the areas in which you will move with comfort. Consider that you need to be able to see the laptop or monitor as you're not facing the big screen. Also, make sure you're not in the middle of the projector's beam and the screen. Arriving on time to the venue will allow you to make arrangements if needed such as moving tables and reconnecting equipment.

2. *Use a clicker.* If you're on a small event, you will likely present from your own laptop, and even though the "stage" is small, using a clicker will give you freedom of movement. With this freedom you can move closer to the audience, or jump between showing slides and whiteboarding, all with ease. In the bigger conferences you will not be allowed to present from your own laptop so the stage manager will give you a clicker. Make sure you get familiar with that type of clicker you're given: practice a few minutes until your mind knows well where each button is.

---

[2]https://unsplash.com/
[3]https://commons.wikimedia.org/wiki/Main_Page

3. *Test both audio and video.* If you need to play audio or video, test them in advance. For videos, the best thing to do is download them and embed them into the presentation so you don't rely on Internet connection. There are tools that allow you to do that, such as youtube-dl.[4] For audio, not only test that it works but make sure the volume level set is loud enough for your audience to get the message you want them to hear.

4. *Never present someone else's slides.* One day you will be asked to replace a speaker on your company or team, and you will be told "Don't worry, the slides are ready, you just have to present." This is a formula for failure, and you should avoid it at all costs. If timing is really tight, at least practice the presentation a couple of times so you will fully review the material and make some of your own adjustments. One of the worst things that can happen is that a folk in the audience asks you "what does this phrase written there mean?" and you have no clue.

# Presentation Hacks from the Masters

Now you know the basics of presentation design and delivery, it's time to learn less-known hacks from the pros in the tech arena. These advanced tactics will make your presentations even more effective and outstanding.

## "New.PPT" by Mikko Hyppönen

Constantly collect screenshots of interesting things that can be used for your future presentations. For instance, when you read, hear something in a podcast, or see an interesting tweet and suddenly feel, *Hey, that's good, that's a good point*, take a note of that even if you have no idea if you can use it in your talks. Have a place on your phone for taking notes. Hyppönen has a slide deck on his computer called "New.PPT" which has grown to gigabytes. So when you see something interesting, make a screenshot, copy/paste, and save it.

When the time comes and you need to prepare material for a new presentation, open "New.PPT" and look at your notes on your phone. You will find a lot of unrelated things, but you could also find the right, hard-to-find piece of content you were looking for. For instance, when you want to show what, for example, a hacked website of a travel agency looks like, you will have a screenshot right there because you saved it six weeks ago when the site was still hacked.

---

[4] https://youtube-dl.org/

Saving things for yourself to use when you need to make new material is useful. As you will always need to update or create new material, you will have good material ready to use.

## "Create As a Comedian" by Mikko Hyppönen

Like many speakers, once Hyppönen creates new material, he reuses part of it for several events. However, at least twice a year he makes a slide deck completely from scratch. Hyppönen listens quite a lot to stand-up comedy, which he recommends to everybody as it can teach you a lot. In interviews with stand-up comedians, many have shared that they do a show, and then they repeat the show with basically the same jokes for six months or so. Then, they throw it in the trash and build a completely new show which doesn't recycle anything. Comedians do this for multiple reasons, partially for their own sanity, and partially because people come back to see their shows. They won't come back in two months, but they might come back in six months or in a year, and if they see a new show, they are happy. Create as a comedian. Twice a year, create all-new slides completely from scratch.

Needless to say, there are exceptions. Some stand-up comedians have jokes that people want to see repeated. It's like the Rolling Stones playing the same songs for decades, or like Hyppönen himself carrying a floppy disk with him onstage for ten years. Both are still demanded.

## "Break Up the Bullet Points" by Kevlin Henney

Kevlin Henney is an independent consultant, speaker, writer, and trainer on software development. He uses one quote, one image, one piece of code, or one diagram per slide, trying to keep it really simple. He knows that you may go through a lot of slides, but each slide has one story and one point to make. So if in the process of creating your slides you find yourself using bullet points, that's immediately a warning sign for you. You need to break it up to more than one slide, or you need to differentiate somehow. Ask yourself, *Do people need to see this or is this just something I'm going to say?*

Henney knows that we go to a lot of talks where there is nothing technically wrong with the information speakers show, but when we see a lot of bullet points we feel overwhelmed and have the impression that the speaker is out of touch. Break up the bullet points.

## "Show Code with Context" by Kevlin Henney

Showing code is common in technical conferences. It can be powerful, but it's always tricky to make it right. Often the problem is just a small font. Speakers want to show code and tend to put a lot of code. The problem is that they're showing a lot of it to fit it all on one screen, and that gives no choice but choosing a very small font size.

Henney has the idea of adjusting. Adjust your story a little bit, acknowledge that all the code is relevant, but for this, you just need to show your audience a small bit rather than showing everything all at once.

A second approach is to break up the code, so tell a story, slide by slide. First, show all of the code in one slide, an overview slide. And then on the next slides, zoom in showing an excerpt of code in a larger font. With this approach, your audience sees a lot of code as a bigger picture, and then you explain the context and emphasize that the key idea is in the smaller excerpt of code.

## "Skip Slides on the Fly" by Kevlin Henney

Henney has learned to finish his talks much more on time than he used to. He recommends we use the presenter mode, where what you see on your laptop is not what people will see on the screen. What they see on the screen is the extended desktop, the second desktop. On your primary desktop, have a clock. By doing this you will have the ability to navigate to other slides. Many people don't realize how many bits you have skipped. People will think you are moving to the next slide but actually, you've just skipped 10 slides in your head. You've already worked out that you won't be able to cover them, they're almost optional, but you can easily control it. Whereas if you present exactly your screen, you don't get that control. This is a useful secret.

Additionally, never use slide numbers because if you put numbers on your slides, people can see where you skip them. Don't enumerate your slides. Otherwise people will notice and think *Hey, wait a minute. He just went from slide 23 to 30*. For Henney, skipping slides on the fly is like a DJ mixing things. The speaker is in charge of that. Henney thinks that sometimes when you give a talk, there is an element of a live show, and sometimes you emphasize a particular aspect, possibly longer than you intended to. It's possible that you're in the middle of a talk and now you have a different way of looking at things. You can then change the content that will be more appropriate for the moment, and simply skip five slides of another topic. So, there is a dynamic element.

## "Slide Velocity" by Kevlin Henney

Another useful skill, especially as you start to give more talks, is to know your slide velocity. If you're using slides, on average how long do you spend per slide?

If suddenly you're concerned about time, this gives you the right order of magnitude and you suddenly realize, *Oh, I'm supposed to speak for 30 minutes, but if I look at my slides that will still take me one hour, clearly that's wrong.* Slide velocity is a matter of awareness. It's like when driving: How fast am I going? What's my typical speed?

## "What If I Am Showing the Wrong Slides?" by Elisa Heikura

Elisa Heikura is a Finnish communications specialist and a coach who wants to make the life of developers and other tech-oriented people so much better—or even easier. One time, Heikura was giving a talk. After about five or ten minutes, she felt that there was something weird on the slides. Some of the data was wrong and she was correcting it while speaking. She realized that she had absolutely the wrong set of slides. What would you do in that situation?

Well, she apologized and informed her audience that she had accidentally chosen the wrong slides from two months ago. So she immediately escaped Keynote and switched the slides. In the meantime, she gave her audience an exercise to interact with the person sitting next while she found her correct slides. They switched their attention away from her until she was ready to continue.

Remember that we are human. Accept that not everything is always perfect and situations like these can happen. Your audience wants you to succeed and will be with you.

## Beyond Presentation Software

This section will tell the stories of two speakers who give presentations but don't use a standard presentation software. First, Soledad Penadés made her own bespoke code to use the web browser to present slides. Second, Horace Dediu uses Perspective app along with his data visualization mastery to create what he calls *cinematic presentations*.

## The Web Browser Is My Presentation Software

In many talks, Soledad Penadés hasn't used any presentation software to make her slides. The browser was enough for her. Penadés motivation to do it was embedding graphical and audio material that Keynote would not allow her to do. In the end, as a passionate coder, she got her hands dirty and built the whole thing herself.

Penadés made two versions. The first was called "minimally viable slide deck"[5] and is based on HTML and CSS. With some simple text and paragraphs, the browser parses that on when you load the slides. The speaker just presses the arrow keys on the keyboard to move to the next or previous slide. The second version, called mindblown.js,[6] was similar, but it would allow you to have all the content in one large website with slides, while also creating 3D content. Both pieces of software are open source, so if you are interested you can look at the code and try it for yourself.

## The World Isn't Ready for Cinematic Presentations

Horace Dediu thinks that the world isn't quite ready yet for cinematic presentations. Dediu presented workshops to teach people how to use Perspective tool, and within those workshops, he explained that whereas the movie industry went from black and white to color, it went from no sound to sound, it went from back projection to green screen, it went from computer-generated graphics and special effects, and now it's using virtual world, as far as presentations are concerned, we're still where the projector was, which gave us the word slide, which was from 1960. Dediu says that we are exactly where we were in the famous scene in *Mad Men* when the Carousel projector was first introduced and they talk about how to advertise it. The word slide comes from the Carousel projector from Kodak which allowed you to project a still photograph, not a negative but a positive color image onto a screen and that is like photography really, showing still photographs. For some reason, even though we ended up with laptops, even though we ended up with tablets, even though we have moved from projectors to LCDs, even though we moved from low resolution to super high resolution, we still have the concept of slides as far as what stands behind a presenter.

As an analyst, as a technology person, Dediu wonders why we can't move forward in the way the visuals are used to support the presenter because if you really have great visuals, the presenter becomes much more comfortable. The presenter becomes much less important in the sense of people judging what's going on because they're just mesmerized by what's on the screen. That shifting of power away from the presenter to the presentation has yet to appear, whether it's in corporate conference rooms or whether it's on the biggest presentation on stage anywhere in the world. We haven't gotten away from photography. We're still images, not cinema. Dediu feels it's perplexing to understand why we can't evolve given the immense technology we have available now.

---

[5]https://github.com/sole/mvsd
[6]https://github.com/sole/mindblown.js

*Chapter 8 | Presentation Hacks*

If you're interested in cinematic presentations, have a look at Perspective[7] app and the Airshow Network.[8] My chapter "Dataviz" in this very book tells stories of how Dediu creates cinematic presentations.

## Key Takeaways

- Slides are not required for every talk and every speaker, even in the tech arena. But if used effectively they can be a valuable tool, as many speakers have shown.
- Where do you start? Start with a pen and paper, and build a storyboard.
- When you have your presentation slides ready, focus on finding the best spot to stand, master the use of a clicker, and pay attention to the audiovisual technicalities to ensure your success.
- Always learn from the masters' best presentation hacks.
- If you feel that standard presentation software is not for you, you can use the browser to present slides, or explore the world of cinematic presentations.

---

[7] http://perspective.pixxa.com/
[8] https://airshow.io/blog

# CHAPTER 9

# Interaction

> *An audience is not brought to you or given to you; it's something that you fight for.*[1]
>
> —Bruce Springsteen, rock singer and songwriter

At the Leetspeak 2014 conference[2] in Gothenburg, independent consultant and entrepreneur Greg Young gave the talk "The Art of Destroying Software."[3] The talk was quite unique in many senses. Young started with two questions in a row. "How many of you have been in a talk about writing code? How many of you have been in a talk about refactoring code?" Until the end of the talk he followed the same dynamic: asking questions. At times he got vocal answers from the audience, or he got hands raised and was able to count them. At times he made them think by raising rhetorical questions such as: "What if you were optimized from the very beginning to be able to delete code?" The ultimate result was a strong interaction with the audience, and he kept their attention high over the 40 minutes. Young's ultimate point was that as a software developer you should optimize your code for deleting, so that any program should be possible to rewrite in one week. The talk, oriented to people who code, was delivered effectively. He even used only two slides, and most of the time he was sitting down at the edge of the stage to be closer to the audience. It was a really interesting talk for its communication, point of view, and for making the audience think, reflect, and interact.

---

[1] Stephanie Sabol. Who Is Bruce Springsteen? Penguin Workshop. 2016.
[2] https://leetspeak.se/2014/
[3] https://vimeo.com/108441214

In contrast, talks on similarly complex topics can come off as boring. They are often flooded with too many slides and the speaker focused only on the screen. No wonder why those talks and their messages are forgotten.

## What Is Audience Interaction?

An ideal scenario for a speaker is that the audience stops being a passive character and becomes an integral part of your story and your talk. When your audience interacts and is engaged, your act becomes like a conversation in which you still have the control. An engaged audience will make you successful.

## How to Interact with Your Audience

Now it's time for you to make sure that audience interaction is an indispensable element of your talks, always on your repertoire. There are different ways you can interact with your audience and engage them. The following is a summary of them.

## Asking Questions

As we saw in Greg Young's talk, one of the simplest and most effective ways to interact with your audience is by asking questions. Something important to be clear about is the reaction you want from the audience. Do you want them to answer by telling you a one-word answer? Do you want them to raise their hands? Do you want them to just silently reflect on your last statement?

When you ask questions and you want an immediate answer, make sure you are clear about that. Give clear instructions. Stillness when you expect answers can have the opposite effect of creating confusion and breaking the dynamic that you were planning.

Some speakers including Heather Wilde call this technique "call and response."[4] The common case is that the speaker interacts, asks questions, and asks people to raise their hands. Call and response is a NLP (neurolinguistic programming) tool too. You will notice this pattern in keynote speakers, the ones that are really good at speaking in public.

A special category is rhetorical questions, which are questions you make without expecting an answer. These are questions asked to make a point rather than to elicit an answer. By asking your question, you want them to

---

[4]https://www.timetoshinepodcast.com/heather-wilde-speaking-in-the-virtual-world

think about a problem, a fact, or an opinion, and by reflecting on that, your audience will be captured and more immersed on the topic of your talk. An example comes from John Chambers' last keynote as Cisco CEO (2015). In that talk he was not only saying goodbye as a CEO but also announcing a big change in the course of the company: embracing digital transformation as a competitive advantage for all Cisco customers and partners. So once Chambers presented all his points, he made a pause and said: "Is this Cisco's strategy, or does it need to be yours?"

A final piece of advice is to make a short pause right after asking the question, just a couple of seconds, so you can let your audience answer or think, before moving to your next line.

## Interactive Polls During the Talk

In recent years, when almost everybody in the audience has a mobile device connected to the Internet, online polls have gained popularity as a way to get an immediate answer from the audience.

It's quite simple. You can share the URL of your poll on your projection or presentation screen and ask your audience to use it. People can quickly type in their browsers and access the poll, vote, and then you can show the results on the big screen.

People will like to participate just for fun or curiosity, and of course being engaged is something everybody wants. As most of these tools produce well-designed visualizations, the audience gets valuable insight as a bonus. Everybody wins.

Some of these tools are IQ Polls,[5] Sendsteps,[6] and Slido.[7]

## Other Tactics for Audience Interaction

In this section, I will share a few final tactics that are beneficial depending on the type of event you are speaking at.

---

[5]https://iqpolls.com/
[6]https://www.sendsteps.com/en/
[7]https://www.sli.do/

## Chapter 9 | Interaction

1. *Keep eye contact.* It's important that your audience has the feeling that you are talking with them. Either because of discomfort or bad habits, many speakers spend a lot of time looking at the floor, their computers, and the presentation screen while ignoring the audience. Get in the habit of looking at specific people in the audience, and from time to time move your eyes across the sections of the audience. Do it until it feels natural.

2. *Interact with a virtual audience.* Nowadays, there are more and more virtual talks, conferences, webinars, which have different audience interaction dynamics. First of all, it's harder to get some response from the audience as you either can't see them or they appear in tiny and low-resolution boxes. Here it is important that you constantly ask for cues, such as "Are you following me?" Also, make sure your eyes are facing the area between the webcam and the center of the computer screen. Otherwise your audience will have the feeling you are not looking at them.

3. *Avoid being behind a lectern.* Some venues have a lectern, podium, or table which often has the speaker's laptop. Unless you really have to type on the computer, such as when you are giving a demo, just stay away from the lectern. Being behind the table creates a barrier between your audience and you. Come to the center and present yourself. Your audience not only came to hear you but to see you too.

4. *Bring the recent moment to your talk.* In the last hours before the talk you experienced many things. You saw something interesting or heard something funny in the conference hall corridor, the speaker before you said a statement that made you reflect, and so on. Make sure you add some of these anecdotes and discoveries to your talk; thus, you will already be involving the current event and the audience will feel engaged in your act.

All in all, there are many strong reasons to interact with your audience, and the best speakers are doing it all the time. Luckily, there are many ways at your disposal to make it happen.

## Key Takeaways

- Audiences like when speakers interact with them, and they will help you succeed as a speaker.
- Asking questions is one of the simplest and easiest ways to effectively interact with your audience.
- Use interactive polls whenever you can. They are easy to arrange and people often enjoy them, and your audience will gain new insights from the results of the poll.
- Learn and practice the mechanics of interacting with a virtual audience.
- Keep eye contact, avoid being behind a lectern, and bring the recent moment to your talk.

# CHAPTER 10

# Staging

*All the world's a stage[1]*

—William Shakespeare

Let's go back in history. The year is 1968. The world was very different from how we know it today. No Internet, no personal computers, no mobile devices. Computers were huge machines that only few people knew how to operate. The crowds believed that computers were to serve corporations and governments, not people. Almost all computer companies and research centers were dedicated to building military technologies. But, in that seemingly dystopian world, a team of computer researchers were preparing something truly amazing.

On December 9, 1968, more than one thousand professionals filled up San Francisco's Brooks Hall to see the unseen. In front of their eyes was a unique work of research, devices, and software created to empower us individuals. The team led by Douglas Engelbart surprised the world by showing the very first videoconference, between San Francisco and Menlo Park, so they could see each other's faces and interact through their computers. This session was part of the ACM/IEEE—Computer Society's Fall Joint Computer Conference—and showed the very first computer mouse, the first hypertext, the first word processor, a collaborative real-time text editor, and many other "firsts." This groundbreaking series of demos, later baptized as The Mother of All Demos,[2] ran almost flawlessly and ended with a standing ovation. It was a show on its own, like a theater play never played again.

---

[1] As You Like It. 2.7.139
[2] https://www.dougengelbart.org/content/view/209/448/

Today, in the 2020s, we have high-definition video, big screens, superfast Internet, virtual reality, high-fidelity audio, and more. These are all amazing technologies that, when put together, can create immersive experiences. However, how often do we see talks with such magnificent staging like the one Engelbart created in 1968? What makes a tech stage feels like a performing arts stage?

## What Is Staging?

When you speak in front of an audience, they not only see you, but they see everything behind you and around you: the big screen, your podium, lectern, microphone stand, the lights, the sounds, all decorations, and how all these elements dynamically follow you during your talk. In other words, it's like a theater play or a concert. Most speakers are not aware of how staging affects their performances and how staging can help make your talk a memorable experience.

Have you ever seen a renowned opera singer singing "La donna è mobile" or "Nessun dorma" while wearing a suit and standing behind a music stand? How do you compare that with the experience of an opera with full costumes, re-created buildings and scenery, and all dynamism across the stage? The difference is tremendous. Think of Cirque du Soleil shows without the staging behind the performers. Yes, extraordinary voices and acrobatic acts are a delight per se, but the staging is what creates the magical experience and transports our minds to the show's imaginary world. On the Ancient Greece, Aristotle called it Spectacle[3] and defined it as one of the six elements for storytelling.

We all can borrow techniques and practices from theater, opera, circus, and movies to rock the tech stage.

## How Engelbart Created a Theater Stage

Engelbart and team could have shown the same series of demos in a back room; they could have projected just their computer screens or the interaction of two team members both in the auditorium. But their innovative instincts told them that a real-time video communication between two locations would have much more impact. They worked on ways to orchestrate such a performance. The result for the audience was seeing several people on different parts of the screen at different times, Engelbart's hands showing the peripherals, and most of the time seeing the computers' screens while the wizard was presenting his astonishing research. They brought a real theater

---

[3]Aristotle. *Poetics*. Cosimo Classics. 2008.

stage, never seen in any computer conference before. This is Aristotle's Spectacle, an artifact that presenters almost never include in their presentation toolkits.

The Mother of All Demos not only brought the computer mouse, showcased the first videoconference, and presented novel data structures for programmers. It also became one of the best presentations in history.

## Speaking at a Cinema

What would be closer to a movie experience for your audience than you speaking at a cinema? Independent consultant Kevlin Henney shared with me that in his long experience as keynote speaker, some conferences are organized at a cinema. That sounds cool, doesn't it? Everybody can see the speaker due to the theater seating (a.k.a. stadium seating) arrangement. The negative aspect is that you as the speaker can't see everybody. Why? Because the lighting is set up against you: all lights are pointing to the stage, while the seats are dark or very dim. Indeed, everybody has comfortable seats and the atmosphere is great. However, if someone asks you a question, you can hear, but not see, that person.

Speaking at a cinema can create fantastic staging for you, but also be prepared for dealing with its potential inconveniences. The best thing you can do is to get in touch with the event producer and ask about lighting. If you want the audience to be lit at some point, tell the technical or production team in advance and they will likely help you arrange that.

## Prepare Yourself for the Stage

You arrived early for the conference and your talk is still a few hours away. Great way to start. Now, what are you going to do during this time? Voxgig CEO Richard Rodger recommends that a speaker should always try to stand on the stage before her talk. So, before your talk, go to the stage. Get up on the stage, look at the room, and create the feeling that the place is already familiar to you. Visualize that your stage time has arrived, and now you have to talk and the audience is there.

Usually, the conference organizers ask speakers to come early and meet them. When you arrive, the technicians will ask you to try your laptop to make sure that is going to work with the audiovisual equipment. Rodger has seen a lot of speakers do this, but they're only focused on getting the audiovisuals right. He recommends that you also take a minute to step away from the computer and let the technicians work so you walk yourself to the middle of the audience and to the middle of the stage, to take in the visual perception and the audio perception. For some this might sound like a strange thing to do, but Rodger finds it very calming.

Arrive early and prepare yourself for the stage. Bear in mind that all your favorite performers do that.

## Staging at the Largest Tech Events

Large companies and organizers of megaconferences take events and staging seriously. Think of events such as CES, E3, Slush, Web Summit, and other similar ones. They create impressive stages that "wow" and inspire their audiences. Some of the most remarkable tech talks and product launches have been executed by two distinct companies. Let's have a look at them.

## Apple Events

A company that has not presented their new products in a small auditorium for nearly two decades is Apple. What you see in every Apple event are huge screens and a real theatrical experience. At the time this book was written in 2020, there is a position listed on the Apple website[4] called *Corporate Events Staging Supervisor* in Cupertino. That gives you an idea of how seriously Apple takes not only event production, but staging as well, and always aims to be ahead in the industry.

## Tesla Product Launches

Another industry that has a predilection for big stages is the automotive sector. Tesla took a step ahead of traditional car companies to create a fresher style, and as you saw in previous chapters, Elon Musk always aims to put on a very creative demo. One time, Musk even used an open-air stage when unveiling details on their SolarCity solar panels.[5] Watch Tesla product launches and pay attention to their stagings so that you can get great ideas for your own events.

## Your Home Is the Stage

If you watch a lot of famous YouTubers to see how they work, you will see that some of them are very good at public speaking, particularly speaking in front of a camera. What makes them good? What's the skill set? This is the skill set you need if you want to make your home the tech stage from which you shine. Richard Rodger has done webinars in which he was speaking to the attendees from his home office or bedroom. The challenge he found is not getting any immediate feedback from an audience. If you can't see the audience, where does the energy come from? Rodger has two main pieces of advice for us:

---

[4] https://www.apple.com/jobs/
[5] https://youtu.be/hMrantzEYC8

1. Watch YouTube videos, listen to podcasts, view good speakers, and take notes. Remember that this is a skill, and skills have to be learned. When you were a child, you could not ride a bicycle. You had to try, sometimes you fell down, but ultimately you learned.
2. Try to attend as many virtual events as possible to get some experience with the audience via screen. Speak, interact, that's your next step. Then give a virtual talk.

Public speaking coach Emily Edgeley has other pieces of advice for speaking virtually from your home:

1. Lighting is key to look professional in front of the camera. Natural lighting is better, so use it whenever possible.
2. As the audience wants to connect with the speaker, show some authenticity. They will be seeing a glance of your house behind you, so show artwork, a bookshelf, or perhaps some plants as your natural background. That will project a bit of your personality without being too distracting.
3. Raise your laptop. Aim to have your eyes at the top of the laptop and your mouth at the center of the screen.

While writing this book the COVID-19 pandemic struck, making these virtual tech stage tips all the more applicable.

## You Can Influence Your Staging

You may be thinking, *I am just a speaker, and even though I wish I had a phenomenal stage to present from, I can't do anything about it.* Yes, you can. In most cases, you can influence the staging for your talk.

If you organize events, take some ideas from this chapter and make the best possible staging based on your resources. Be creative.

If you are invited to speak at events, you can always ask the event production team or event organizer what type of screens are available, whether the venue is theater style, what the options are for lighting, and much more.

## Best Practices

- Aristotle wrote there are six rules of storytelling.[6] One of them is especially applicable to us here today and can make you a phenomenal presenter. Create a theater stage by bringing *Spectacle* where appropriate. Props and a stage background can add a lot to your presentation. In the most acclaimed movies, *Spectacle* includes the technical special effects. However, you don't need expensive equipment to create special effects, as you can make them happen with audience participation and simple tricks to utilize the energy of the room.

- If you are showing presentation slides, photos, or anything else to be displayed on a screen, make sure they are a 16 × 9 proportion. This is the most common standard today and creates a long horizontal view. A few years ago the preferred format was 4 × 3, but preference has shifted.

- Define a theme for your talk. Make all visuals and colors align to that theme. For instance, if your theme is nature, you can ask the event producer to use green lights and some available scenery. Even at a small event, you can usually ask the venue owner for simple props, and often you can choose the type of chairs for your audience. Every single detail will help you to set the atmosphere you want.

- A trend in recent years is huge screens. These are not in fact single massive screens, but instead what is called a "video wall."[7]

---

[6]Aristotle. *Poetics*. Cosimo Classics. 2008.
[7]https://onsign.tv/tutorials/how-to-build-a-video-wall/

## Key Takeaways

- Staging is part of your performance and makes a big impact on it.

- Watch talks that have great staging, pay attention to details, and find inspiration for your own events and performances. Particularly, Apple and Tesla stand out of the crowd.

- Prepare yourself for the stage. Arrive at the venue early and spend time both on the stage and in the audience area.

- Today, your home can be the stage. Build the skills to speak in front of a camera and to interact with a virtual audience. Create your own stage and add your personality to it.

# CHAPTER 11

# Memory

> *An amateur practices until he can get it right. A professional practices until he can't get it wrong.*
>
> —Anonymous

On November 22, 2018, at Kulttuuritalo concert hall in Helsinki, F-Secure Chief Research Officer Mikko Hyppönen was in the middle of a talk at the Hack\Talks 2018 conference.[1] He said, "Smart phone, vulnerable phone. Smart watch, vulnerable watch. Smart cars, smart city, smart grid..." when someone in the audience spoke out loud and said, "Smart projectors!"

What was happening?

The projector had actually stopped working. Hyppönen looked back toward the big screen and said, "Oh, I see." He then continued speaking, but without slides. He didn't waste even a few seconds and continued talking for eight minutes until the problem was fixed. The projector was back up and running, and he continued with the subsequent slides. Yes, it was eight minutes without the slides he had prepared. Impressive. That is the result of both experience and preparation, and a speaker knowing his material really well.

---

[1] https://youtu.be/uZwrnT9zDtw

© Oscar Santolalla 2020
O. Santolalla, *Rock the Tech Stage*, https://doi.org/10.1007/978-1-4842-6312-9_11

## Chapter 11 | Memory

In this chapter, we will discuss the importance of using your memory when preparing yourself for your talk. We will discuss how much we can rely on memory and ask some questions: Should you learn your content by heart? Should you use notes? What about a teleprompter? All this and more will be answered.

## Remembering Your Lines

There is no single answer for how to best remember your lines. Every person is different, every talk is different. Let's explore some of the most known options:

1. *Rehearse a lot.* This is the simplest and most effective way to remember your lines. After a lot of practice you reach a point in which the lines come easily and you can improvise and appear spontaneous. It doesn't necessarily imply learning by heart.

2. *Learn by heart.* You set the clear goal of knowing your talk word for word. First, you have to write a script that you will stick to. Naturally, you need to rehearse an extraordinary amount of time until you can't get it wrong. Improvisation is not allowed. This is the way professional actors do learn their scripts.

3. *Use notes.* This is a supporting memory device, in which you write a very short list of words (or objects) that typically include key phrases and the structure of your talk. Notes look the best when they are in small firm paper (like cards), instead of a full letter or A4 size sheet.

4. *Use a teleprompter.* An electronic device often seen at big events. Use them with care, as will be further explained later in this chapter.

5. *Use advanced memory techniques.* There are memory techniques that anchor every segment of your talk with a visual object that is easy to remember. Once you memorize the sequence of objects, you can remember the flow and key structure of your talk.

All in all, for most of the talks on your professional life, the best combination is to **rehearse a lot** and **use notes** if you feel you need them.

## Should You Learn a Speech by Heart?

There has been a continuous debate around if a speaker should learn their lines by heart. And this debate will continue with strong arguments on both sides.

ROCeteer CTO Heather Wilde gave me an enlightening answer when I asked her *How do you achieve good memory?* Wilde expressed the advice that one should never get on stage unless they have ten times the amount of information as the length of one's own talk. Such accumulated knowledge and all the experiences lived with the topic will help the speaker overbear any potential problem. Whatever people ask you, you know it.

I couldn't agree more, and her point is not only about memorizing your presentation material, but the fact that you need to know *a lot* about the speaking topic in order to have that comfortable memory. The reason why many speakers struggle to memorize their lines is because they don't know enough about the topic. Avoid that situation by choosing topics you know very well.

Interestingly, when you ask how to give good talks, some people recommend TED and TEDx talks as a paradigm. Such talks are great for getting ideas and inspiration. However, these talks are a once-in-a-lifetime opportunity to speak—a highlight of your career—and for that occasion you need an outstanding amount of preparation. For such talks which are scheduled several months ahead of time, yes, I recommend you to learn the lines by heart and rehearse it dozens of times. But then again, these are exceptions to the rule for any professional. Most of the talks you will give will be in internal meetings, workshops, meetups, technical conferences, and ad hoc situations in which you will have limited time to practice.

## A Trick to Hide Your Notes

Mikko Hyppönen shared with me a special trick he has done with notes. If you remember Chapter 7, we have seen the power of props. Hyppönen was speaking at the Slush 2019 conference in Helsinki, and his talk was titled "Why AI Will Be Inhuman."[2] He talked about artificial intelligence, and he said that he heard the term for the first time in 1983 while reading a computer magazine. So as he said that, he showed an original copy of a 1983 issue of *Tekniikan Maailma*[3] (a computer magazine in Finnish) with said article. That was a nice prop to illustrate his point, giving a nostalgic touch. For the rest of the talk, he walked around the stage with the magazine. It was a talk with very few slides, and in many sections he spoke with slides that didn't contain any text.

So, where were his notes?

---

[2] https://vimeo.com/374914179
[3] https://tekniikanmaailma.fi/

The notes were hidden on the back cover of the magazine. He printed the keywords and the structure of his talk and stapled it on the back cover. If you observe the video carefully, you can notice moments when he looks at the notes. At times he showed the audience the magazine simply so that he could take a look again. However, for the audience, it was really hard to spot that Hyppönen was using notes. While sharing this story with me, he acknowledged he didn't remember the whole talk by heart but also emphasized he didn't need to.

## The Risk of Becoming a Teleprompter Reader

Especially at large conferences, we see top executives of large brands speaking from a teleprompter (a.k.a. an autocue). This is a very common practice at such events.

A teleprompter is a device that shows the speaker's upcoming text a few lines at a time, then moving on to the next lines. Today, politicians use glass teleprompters that are nearly invisible to the audience. Though it might look like a safe choice—if your company or event organizer can afford it—the best thing is to avoid a teleprompter unless you are already really good at it. Leave the teleprompter for a bigger speech, when you have to speak a text word for word.

Movie director Michael Bay appeared at CES 2014 backing up Samsung smart TVs. Unfortunately for him, the teleprompter failed[4] shortly after he started speaking, and it made it evident that Bay didn't really know his lines well. At first Bay said, "The type is all off. Sorry. But I'll just wing this," but he felt so nervous that he quickly left the stage in an unfinished and odd act.

I have seen so many large companies' speakers reading from the autocue, which I find it hard to understand. In contrast, you will not find a video in which you see Steve Jobs reading from a teleprompter. Jobs really knew the power of rehearsal and internalizing his content to speaking free style.

Using a teleprompter can give you a false sense of security. A teleprompter—like any memory device—can fail, so be aware of that.

---

[4] https://youtu.be/ch9hWO4UYYk

## How Many Times Does a World Champion of Public Speaking Rehearse?

Every year, Toastmasters International[5] organizes a competition called the World Championship of Public Speaking. More than 30,000 people around the globe compete in several levels until a grand final arranged during an international convention which is usually in August. In my experience as a podcast host of my show Time to Shine, I had the opportunity to interview not only a few of these champions but also speaking coaches who have closely worked with contestants for the final. When I asked them how many times a winner rehearsed, the answer was between 100 and 200 times. That's an impressive number which shows how these speakers achieve such precision and how the speeches become inspiring and entertaining for anybody who watches them.

An example from our field in the tech industry is system analyst Mohammed Qahtani who became world champion in 2015 with the speech "The Power of Words."[6] The storyline of this fantastic speech started with fine humor and ended with dramatic lines, a script that required great performance precision to achieve the desired impact in the audience. Qahtani not only showed us the power of words but the power of rehearsal.

## Key Takeaways

- Practice your lines as much as you can. That is the best way to help your memory.
- For the overwhelming majority of the talks you will give, you don't have to know your lines by heart.
- Use notes if you feel you need them.
- Speak topics you know very well.

---

[5]https://www.toastmasters.org/about/all-about-toastmasters
[6]https://youtu.be/qasE4ecA57Y

# CHAPTER 12

# The Virtual Tech Stage

Starting in February 2020, we began to hear how conferences were going to be canceled because of COVID-19; the first of these announcements came from the Mobile World Congress.[1] Then in March, the pandemic was declared and all conferences fell apart like a house of cards. Many were canceled or postponed until the following year. The ones that had a bit more time for preparations went virtual for their very first time. Similarly, all types of business internal meetings massively became virtual. Easy as it might sound, most people were not ready for this switch from in-person to virtual. How can we present effectively in the virtual world?

## A Virtual Conference Made Different

A venerated conference in the tech world is Apple Worldwide Developers Conference. This year WWDC 2020[2] took place from June 22 to 26, and for the first time it was completely online. Apple orchestrated the event very well, setting a standard to be met by others in the industry.

---

[1] https://www.gsma.com/newsroom/press-release/gsma-statement-on-mwc-barcelona-2020/
[2] https://www.apple.com/apple-events/june-2020/

© Oscar Santolalla 2020
O. Santolalla, *Rock the Tech Stage*, https://doi.org/10.1007/978-1-4842-6312-9_12

## Chapter 12 | The Virtual Tech Stage

The event started with Apple CEO Tim Cook speaking at an empty Steve Jobs Theater in their headquarters. From there onward several Apple executives appeared presenting different sections of the keynote for a total of 1 hour and 48 minutes. They appeared either inside the Apple headquarters building in Cupertino or in other locations, both indoors and outdoors. That gave the event an additional feeling of dynamism so the viewers wouldn't get bored seeing the same stage background over and over. That pre-recorded video kick-started five days full of technical sessions that allowed developers to learn in depth the innovations announced throughout the keynote.

From information that the media has collected,[3] it felt like attendees liked the arrangements beyond the pre-recorded virtual presentations. Particularly, developers were delighted with the consultation sessions arranged to have one-on-one conversations with the right Apple specialist.

All in all, great production and creative ways to make a virtual conference different made the event a success.

## Benefits of Virtual Conferences

Let's look at the advantages that virtual conferences have over their in-person counterparts:

- Ease of access for those who travel is difficult for. You can attend the conference from anywhere.

- More affordable for attendees. The more renowned conferences cost more than 1000 USD. And either the attendees or their companies have to incur travel costs too.

- More opportunities to speak, as the physical barriers are gone. As a speaker you can give a keynote or a technical session to a conference on another continent, in places you have never been before.

- The production can fix glitches. As you know, technology fails from time to time: presentation software, a demo, or Internet connection. The production team can make sure the video is taken again and edited until they create a flawless final product.

---

[3]https://www.wsj.com/articles/apples-virtual-event-gives-hope-for-online-only-conferences-in-covid-19-era-11593553261

# How to Be Effective in Virtual Presentations

Speaking in virtual events is similar to speaking in-person in many aspects but is different in other aspects too. Let's first distinguish these differences.

Table 12-1. Speaking in the virtual world vs. speaking in-person

| Speaking in the virtual world | Speaking in-person |
| --- | --- |
| There is no direct feedback and interaction with the audience. You can't see their faces, hear their reactions, and get immediate answers. | By default you can see everything your audience does and says. The exception is in very large events with thousands of attendees. |
| You are speaking to a camera, which requires different skills. | You are speaking to the audience that is in front of you. |
| You as a speaker are responsible for the stage, lighting, sound, background, room acoustics, etc. | The event organizer is responsible for the stage, lighting, sound, etc. |
| Difficult to make attendees interact with the others. | Easy to tell them ask a question to and discuss with the person sitting next to you. |
| People get tired and anxious to listen for a long period. | People are used to sit and listen to a speaker for one hour and several talks in a row. |

As you can see in Table 12-1, your presentations have to adapt to the virtual world. One of the main aspects is length. You have to speak shorter and give more.

# Main Skills to Learn or Improve

Now it's time to identify the skills that we have to improve and the new skills we need to learn.

## Videoconferencing Tools

The first names that people have in mind when hearing videoconferencing tools are Skype and Zoom. For both enterprise and all-purpose there are several tools that you could use to build the whole virtual presentation experience: GoToMeeting, Microsoft Teams, Cisco Webex, and others. As most of these services offer a free trial, the best is that you try a few of these tools and see which one fits your need the best.

Once you have chosen a tool, invest time in learning the features beyond the basics. Not only you will discover very useful features such as breakout rooms, polls, marketing tools, integration with other services, but you will also be ready to solve problems yourself when things go out of script. Especially, learn well how to use your videoconferencing tool together with your presentation software.

Fantastic as all these tools are, use as little technology as possible. This will minimize the risks of failure.

## Speak in Front of a Camera

This isn't new as some people already had opportunities to be interviewed for the TV, a video podcast, run YouTube channels, and so on. However, for most people, this was an occasional activity to do. Now speaking in front of a camera is the default.

When you are speaking in an auditorium or meeting room, your eyesight will be moving from different persons in the room, some very close to you, others far. Sometimes you will look at the whole audience without fixing your attention to any person. Now you must look at the camera all the time and make your gestures pointing toward the camera too. If you look outside the camera for just a few seconds, the audience will notice it as a distraction.

This is why it's very important that the camera is approximately at your eye level.

If possible, stand up while you speak. First of all, you will stand out as most speakers will speak sitting on a couch or a desk chair. After all, speaking while walking is the way you do it for in-person talks, so it should be more natural.

## Set Your Own Stage

In face-to-face events, the conference organizer is responsible for the venue: they have rented the room, set up lighting, sound, microphones, decorated the stage, installed whiteboard, flipcharts, and so on. Now from your house you are the one responsible to create a stage that looks professional and reflects your personality and the theme of your talk.

Just think of virtual meetings you have participated in or even screenshots shared on the net in which you saw a grid of all participants' faces. What you often see is: too dark, the light comes too bright from one side, messy rooms on the background, poor contrast between the speaker's wear and her background colors, and so on. Certainly the vast majority of people were not prepared to use remote meetings and just did their best to use the tool and get the things done.

How to control the virtual stage? There are two main elements to pay attention: the background and lighting.

*Background.* Here you have two main options: virtual background or real background. Whether you choose one or the other, the most important things that the background needs are

- It looks professional.
- It matches the theme of your message.
- It's not distracting.

All videoconferencing tools allow you to use virtual backgrounds, and additionally you can find many sites that offer free backgrounds.[4]

When using virtual backgrounds you might notice that when the speakers move, the edges show part of the real background. Even sometimes you appear headless. This occurs because the videoconferencing tool fails to distinguish between you and the real background behind you. In order to mitigate this, a step forward is to mount a green screen[5] behind you, which is a technique used in movies. The reason why these screens are green—and not another color—is because that's a rare color used in people's clothes.

Some tools like Microsoft Teams can blur your real background, which is an alternative between virtual and real backgrounds.

However, showing a real background gives an even better impression. People want to see the real world behind you and not have the impression you are hiding something. Arrange your background to show your personality: show some artwork, a bookshelf, plants, anything that looks good and shows your ethos.

*Lighting.* The utmost of all principles for lighting is: use sunlight whenever possible. Sunlight is the most natural and most pleasant lighting. But sunlight can be too bright and spoil your video shots, a challenge that photographers often face. Ensure you have good front light, so people will see your face nicely lit, not shady. Don't be with your back to an open window as you will look dark. The opposite is the best, be behind an area that is lit by the sun frontally, neither laterally nor diagonally. That will give the sense that your face and body are lit in a natural way.

---

[4]https://www.tomsguide.com/news/best-free-zoom-backgrounds
[5]https://www.techsmith.com/blog/how-to-create-a-diy-green-scre/

When sunlight isn't an option, you need to invest in some lighting sets. There is a world of lighting on its own, which is beyond the scope of this book. The main goal is still making sure your face is lit frontally in a natural way. To achieve this with artificial light, you will need a set of lamps, stands to place them in the right place to point you, and diffusion filters. Thanks to the high demand for this know-how, you will find many resources online[6] to learn and try until you find a lighting set that meets your needs.

## Voice

When you speak in a virtual event, your voice will be different from how your audience would hear you in a conference room. This is affected by several factors: the microphone, Internet connection, the acoustics of the room you are in, and also how you hear your own voice on the headphones. A key element is the awareness of your own voice, *do you know how your voice sounds?* You might have noticed people speaking either too loud or too quiet as a result of how they hear themselves in their earphones. I strongly recommend you practice with the setup you will use for the virtual event, record yourself with your smartphone, and hear that audio recording. That will help you to adjust your voice.

Your audience will follow you more if you sound dynamic, enthused. You might remember the previous chapter about passion. In virtual events attendees tend to be more distracted but they can't ignore a speaker who speaks with energy.

Regarding microphones, there are many possibilities: some webcams have incorporated mics, headsets (both wired and wireless), an external microphone on your desk, and so on. If you stand up and move, a wireless lavalier is attached to your jacket. The aim is to have the microphone the closest to your mouth, that is how you'll get the best sound.

For live events, there is a chance that the connection becomes unstable, so speak slower and emphasize your speech melody. In pre-recorded events you can speak at a faster tempo.

All in all, if you can choose a single piece of advice which will enrich your voice in virtual events is this: speak loud.

---

[6]https://www.techsmith.com/blog/get-perfect-lighting-video/

## Interaction in the Virtual World

Speaking in public isn't a unidirectional communication act, it's an interaction. One of the main hardships speakers find in virtual presentations is the lack of interaction, not getting feedback from the audience is very hard. Sometimes you might not even know if the people are hearing you and seeing you. Chapter 9 "Interaction" already delved into the challenges of audience interaction, but for the virtual world in particular:

1. Walking around the stage is also a style that will make your presentation more interactive. As most speakers will be sitting and showing only their faces, you will stand out and make your video footage more dynamic. Standing will also give you more room for making hand gestures and showing props. People will see less of PowerPoint, more of a human.

2. Use online interactive polls such as Mentimeter[7] and Poll Everywhere.[8] They can be integrated with the videoconferencing tools or the presentation software. If you use polls a few times across your talk, you will keep your audience active. At their best, these tools will show the polls' results with such amazing dataviz that your audience will not help but taking screenshots or capturing a photo of their screens.

# Conferences Won't Be the Same in the Short Term

As you saw from Apple's example, conference organizers already started to create remote-only experiences. Consumer Technology Association has announced that CES 2021 will be all-digital (see Figure 12-1). CES organizers already predict that some of the virtual world will continue in the years to come: "We plan to return to Las Vegas for CES 2022, combining the best elements of a physical and digital show."[9] So the virtual stage is not a trend but part of the new way companies and event organizers will run the shows in the future.

Some innovations in the event industry are the use of virtual trade shows, with virtual booths in which both exhibitors and attendees can still feel the booth experience: see a demo with the latest technologies, and even sign contracts. Virtual reality booths go a step farther.

---

[7]https://www.mentimeter.com/
[8]https://www.polleverywhere.com/
[9]https://www.ces.tech/planning-for-ces-2021.aspx

Organizers are also offering one of the main reasons a person would pay the hefty ticket price: asking questions or talking with a renowned speaker. This is arranged in either private or small group virtual meetings.

More and more innovations will come, so if you are also an event organizer, attend virtual events regularly and grasp ideas from the best in the industry.

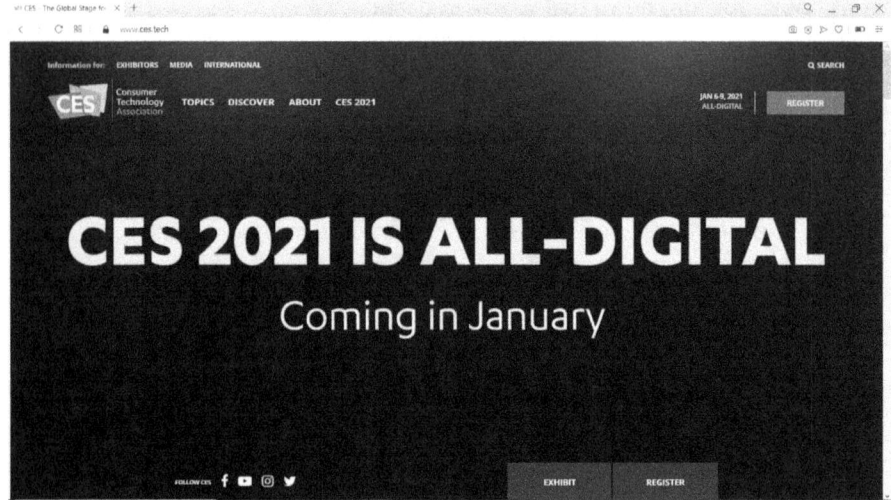

**Figure 12-1.** CES 2021 is all-digital

The virtual tech stage is here to stay, so you need to be well prepared for it. It's time to learn some new skills, try new things. Exciting times ahead.

# CHAPTER 13

# Get Started!

The secrets of rocking the tech stage are now revealed to you. Now you know how the best speakers in the business do their magic. Naturally, other techies communicate effectively in smaller events such as meetups, team meetings, internal meetings, town halls, webinars, and more.

You may be asking yourself, *Where do I start?* This final chapter is especially for people who haven't started to speak on the tech stage yet. But if you are already active, this can give you useful ideas too.

## What If I Have Impostor Syndrome?

Something that has prevented people from speaking in public is impostor syndrome. Impostor syndrome is a psychological condition that is characterized by persistent doubt concerning one's abilities or accomplishments accompanied by the fear of being exposed as a fraud despite evidence of one's ongoing success.[1] In other words, is the fear that at any time someone will reveal that you are a fraud, that you don't know what you are talking about, that you are not competent, or that you don't know your job well. The truth is that this feeling is extremely common and especially among highly competent people. Elisa Heikura said[2] that almost every software developer suffers from impostor syndrome and the reason is that everything in their world is in constant

---

[1] Merriam-Webster Dictionary, https://www.merriam-webster.com/dictionary/impostor%20syndrome syndrome, Accessed 16 Aug. 2020.
[2] https://www.timetoshinepodcast.com/elisa-heikura-can-we-overcome-impostor-syndrome/

change: the technologies, the programming languages, development tools, and so on. It's ironic because many people are extremely competent and brilliant and have amazing stories to tell. But because of impostor syndrome they think that they have to be perfect and that if they make a mistake onstage that will be the end of their careers.

As a palliative, Heikura suggests that people build a service attitude. Imagine you are preparing yourself for a talk. Now, turn the focus to the audience. Ask yourself the questions, *What am I giving? What is the main key takeaway of the speech?*

And then, when you have the essence of the speech, depending on how much time you have, think about the questions, *How will I make them remember? How will I make them understand? How will I make them see the point? Why should they be interested? Why should they remember?*

The speech builds naturally from those questions because when you first have the essence of the topic, you will have the why, the opening, and confidence with how you're going to persuade the audience to agree with your message. And then when you think about how you're going to make them remember you will find stories, case examples, demos, quotes, data, and more.

All in all, switching your focus to the audience and how your message will help and serve them is a formula that will empower you. It will eventually convince you that you have a mission, and to fulfill your mission you must go to the stage and share your story.

# Find a Great Topic

If you now want to start speaking, one of the first questions you could be asking yourself is, *What topic do I speak about?* Don't worry. Every single speaker has had the same experience. It can take some time to explore and decide your speaking topics. The three main elements that can help you define your topic are

1. In what topic do you have knowledge that others don't? For instance, you might be working with a technology, product, or tool that very few people do. If you have developed a high expertise that others don't have, it's perceived valuable for people working with the same topic.

2. What are your genuine interests, both professionally and personally? The word *passion* often comes up here. If you are an entrepreneur and you want to promote your product, passion is key.

3. You might have special opinion about something. There could be a popular topic, in which many people already talk about it, but if you have a different, unique opinion or perspective about it, then that is the value you can share. If your points are thought-provoking and interesting, people will listen to you.

These are the three starting points to create topics: knowledge, interests, and opinions.

## Bloggers First

Some speakers have started taking a different path. They became active bloggers for some time before starting to speak, either for their companies or in their own professional blogs. Soledad Penadés, Horace Dediu, and many other speakers started blogging. In Penadés' case, she started writing about coding from 2004[3] and her busiest time as a speaker in the tech stage only arrived in 2013.[4]

By blogging consistently, after some time you will have created and accumulated valuable content which can be more easily transformed into a talk, and you will have established a name as an expert in your field. That reputation can already help you find places to speak and be recognized as an authority in the matter.

## Applying for Conferences

Let's say that now you have a topic, have already spoken a couple of times either at work or elsewhere, but now you don't know where to speak next. What should you do? A few options you can combine are

1. *Research the web.* Open your favorite search engine and add the keywords "call for speakers" plus other specific information such as your city, country, the year, and obviously the topic. Other useful keywords are "speaker submission," "speaker submission form," which can be combined with "conference" or "meetup." To go a step further, many search engines allow you to set alerts so you will receive email notifications when new results are indexed. In addition to this, LinkedIn, Twitter, and most social media platforms allow you to follow hashtags such as #callforspeakers.

---

[3]https://soledadpenades.com/posts/
[4]https://soledadpenades.com/speaking/

2. *Talk to more experienced colleagues or friends who already speak in conferences.* Networking is key. They might have insider information, such as conferences that haven't been announced publicly yet.

3. *Make a short list of speakers you have seen or heard in your field of interest.* Search their names and learn about the conferences they have spoken at before. That will produce you a list of potential conferences in the countries or regions you are targeting that share your interests.

4. *Pitch yourself.* Conference organizers will judge if you are suitable for speaking on their event. As a new speaker they can't expect you have a speaker's web page, but they want to see what you are doing and what you have done in your field. This is why it is crucial that you keep your online presence up to date and with a professional look, especially LinkedIn (or the equivalent professional platform on your region). You also need to have a pitch of yourself (normally called Bio) ready to be sent in a submission form. The Bio must depict your experience and skills but also two important things:

    - *Your motivation.* Tell them why you are passionate about your field, and why this particular conference will benefit with your presence.

    - *A personal touch.* Tell them who you are beyond your professional persona, *are you fond of heavy metal, volleyball, hiking, astronomy?* Share some of your interests, especially the ones that have a connection with the theme of the conference.

    Three or four sentences is enough, this is not a CV. Keep your Bio short and simple, but also intriguing.

5. *Pitch your topic.* I already shared ideas on how to find great topics. Now it's time to convince conference organizers that your topic must be written on the agenda. List the benefits that your topic will bring to the audience, and make sure the title expresses it and calls the attention. The more specific a topic the better.

## A Tool for Speakers in Tech

Richard Rodger shared with me that when he became an active speaker, he was representing his former company in conferences at least two or three times a month. With that speaking frequency, a considerable amount of his time was spent in preparations for speaking. First, a speaker has to apply up to six months in advance for a conference and has to send a proposal to speak or get invited. As you can imagine, each conference has a different application form. Once accepted, the speaker has to plan everything, and at the same time synchronizing with their marketing or sales teams. For instance, putting up tweets so that people know you're going to be speaking is helpful. Another point to consider is how to make sure your speaker's page, either on a personal blog or the company's website, is up to date. The weeks pass by, the conference approaches, and the organizers will start to ask you about your arrival times, dietary preferences, and more. You have to be prepared and easy to work with. There is a lot of friction in the workflow and execution around being a speaker.

To solve this, Rodger first tried with a spreadsheet to organize everything and later tried to use different services from project management to event management tools. Nothing worked well.

In the end, Rodger decided to scratch his own itches and build a software to fix this problem. He created voxgig,[5] a service that aims to make things very easy for both speakers and event organizers and is especially focused in the tech arena.

In voxgig's model, the users are the speakers and the customers are the companies that the speakers work for. Some big tech companies have developer evangelists, whose job is to go to conferences and speak about their API services and similar topics. Large companies might have more than 100 developer evangelists, so you can imagine the challenges organizing it all brings.

Now voxgig is on a private beta mode of invite only. Rodger is obsessive in terms of wanting to make it a good experience, so the tool looks like a promised land for speakers in tech.

A fantastic vision. Coming soon, stay tuned.

---

[5]https://www.voxgig.com/

## Having a Talk Is Not the End Goal

Developer and speaker Soledad Penadés told me that throughout her experience she has seen many people who go to a conference, make friends with the speakers, and automatically want to be a speaker after seeing a few they enjoyed. Then, their obvious challenge is to figure out what they should talk about. They don't even know what they want to talk about, but rather just want to be speakers. On the one hand, it's fantastic to know that some speakers inspire others to follow their path to become speakers too, but on the other hand, I agree with Penadés. *Having a talk is not the end goal.* The end goal is to communicate something and teach something to people. So, if you are inspired to speak, find what you want to talk about and then talk about that thing. Start small, share your knowledge, share value, and share your stories.

## Beware of Scams

Cybercriminals attack web shoppers, big corporations, and governments, but it was only when I spoke with F-Secure Chief Research Officer Mikko Hyppönen that I learned they also target conference speakers. Hyppönen told me that in late 2019 and early 2020 he was contacted by two different scammers. This is how they operate against speakers. A person contacts you via email directly posing as someone else, a real person. *Hello, I've worked for the son of the crown Prince of the United Arab Emirates. We're setting up a charity event. We would like to hire you to speak about artificial intelligence and data security.* They offer you whatever you ask for as a fee, paid flights and expenses. The event—which doesn't exist at all—has a professional-looking website.

And there the scam comes. The way they make money out of this is that first they offer you €20,000 for the speaker keynote gig. But then later, they get back to you with something like, *We're actually starting a new charity. We're looking for publicity for this new charity. We would like to kick it off by getting a group of celebrities donating money to our charity. We pay you extra €5,000 if you donate that €5,000 to our charity. We'd make a press release about it, which makes you look good and makes us look good.*

And then they pay you the actual money, €20,000 plus €5,000. That amount is paid through a mechanism they can withdraw (like a stolen credit card) which gets canceled. During the window when you got the money, you pay the €5,000 to their charity. Once you've paid it, you've fallen for the scam, and your €5,000 are gone. The €25,000 gets withdrawn and you are €5,000 in the red, suddenly the event website is gone, and you realize there's no event at all. The criminals have a very limited time window to make the fraud, and some people have fallen into this scam.

Be aware that this is happening.

## Some Final Advice

I had the privilege of talking with truly interesting people in the tech arena during the time of writing this book and beforehand. And I would like to end with two ideas that go beyond the preparation for your talks.

### You've Got to Have a Mentor

The most successful people you have seen share something in common: they have had mentors throughout their lives. So Heather Wilde's extra piece of advice is, "You've got to have a mentor." Wilde has spoken many times in talks and interviews[6] about having a mentor. I couldn't agree more with her and I can tell it from my own personal experience.

### Keep Your Hands Dirty

When you become a good speaker and have achieved a leadership position, should you stop coding and being technical?

Mikko Hyppönen thinks that a good speaker in tech has to keep their hands dirty, which means you have to do the actual work yourself. Typically the career path for technical experts is such that the longer they've been in their field, the more they end up doing managerial things, and speaking about the technology instead of actually doing the technology. Vice presidents or CTOs of technology companies don't code anything anymore. But if you want to be a credible technical expert, you have to do this work by yourself as well. You have to test the systems. You have to be able to install a Docker environment in a cloud storage and bring it up, for example. You have to be able to write code. You have to be able to reverse engineer other people's code if you want to be a credible expert in that area. So, you have to take the time and get your hands dirty, even if you don't need to.

Otherwise you will one day find that you are on a keynote stage speaking about topics that you don't actually understand anymore. That's not where you want to be.

---

[6] https://youtu.be/sMAP4lk_0-k

## Now, Get Out and Speak!

I have been in the technology industry nearly two decades, and in my journey I have seen it from many different perspectives: as an entrepreneur, researcher, technical specialist, product manager, in sales, and now as a sales engineer. As much as I have been inspired and influenced by companies and products, I have been inspired by their spokespeople. The ones who took the mic and went to the stage to amplify their ideas. From all that I have seen in the tech arena, there is something always in the air: passion.

If you have passion in your product and technology, and if you want your technology to make a big impact in society, make sure to not only build great technology and products, but to speak about them loudly.

Now, get out and speak. Rock the tech stage.

**APPENDIX A**

# Resources

This additional section provides you a wider list of resources that will help you put into practice the advice from this book.

## For Further Reading

American rhetoric https://www.americanrhetoric.com/

*Create and Deliver a Killer Product Demo*, Oscar Santolalla https://www.apress.com/gp/book/9781484239537

*Effective Data Visualization: The Right Chart for the Right Data 2nd Edition*, Stephanie Evergreen

*Find Your Voice: The Secret to Talking with Confidence in Any Situation*, Caroline Goyder

*Made to Stick: Why Some Ideas Survive and Others Die*, Chip Heath and Dan Heath

*Pitching For Life*, Walid O. El Cheik. https://www.pitchingforlife.com/

*Presentation Zen: Simple Ideas on Presentation Design and Delivery (3rd Edition)*, Garr Reynolds

*The Presentation Secrets of Steve Jobs*, Carmine Gallo

© Oscar Santolalla 2020
O. Santolalla, *Rock the Tech Stage*, https://doi.org/10.1007/978-1-4842-6312-9

# Appendix A | Resources

## Useful Online Tools

Interactive Chart Chooser https://depictdatastudio.com/charts/

Canva's Online storyboard maker https://www.canva.com/create/storyboards/

Voxgig https://www.voxgig.com/

## Applications

Cinematic Presentations

Perspective app http://perspective.pixxa.com/

Interactive Polls

IQ Polls https://iqpolls.com/

Mentimeter https://www.mentimeter.com/

Poll Everywhere https://www.polleverywhere.com/

Sendsteps https://www.sendsteps.com/en/

Slido https://www.sli.do/

For Windows

ZoomIt https://docs.microsoft.com/en-us/sysinternals/downloads/zoomit

Other Utilities

youtube-dl https://youtube-dl.org/

## Podcasts

Fireside with Voxgig for Professional Speakers https://podcasts.apple.com/gb/podcast/fireside-with-voxgig-for-professional-speakers/id1439330890

The Present Beyond Measure Show https://podcasts.apple.com/us/podcast/present-beyond-measure-show-data-visualization-storytelling/id1029765276

Time to Shine https://www.timetoshinepodcast.com/

## Online Galleries for Photos

Pexels https://www.pexels.com/

Pixabay https://pixabay.com/

Unsplash https://unsplash.com/

Wikimedia Commons https://commons.wikimedia.org

Zoom backgrounds https://www.tomsguide.com/news/best-free-zoom-backgrounds

## Public Speaking Training

Toastmasters International https://www.toastmasters.org/

# Index

## A
Audience interaction
  asking questions, 78
  defining, 78
  polls, 79
  tactics, 79, 80
Augmentation Research Center (ARC), 15

## B
Blogs, 107

## C
Cisco's method, 5
CityPass mobile app, 5
Conferences, applying
  having talk is not end goal, 110
  options, 107, 108
  scams, 110
  speaker in tech, tool, 109

## D, E, F, G, H
Data visualization
  blue square, map, 39, 40
  charts, 34, 36
  cinematic presentations, 44, 45
  communicate idea, 40–44
  complex types, 34
  definition, 34
  present data effectively, 46, 47
  presenting data, mistakes, 37, 38
  startup pitches, 48

## I, J
Impostor syndrome, 2, 105, 106

## K, L
Killer demos
  API demos, 13, 14
  embeddings, 20
  iPhone launch (2007), 16
  Macintosh launch (1984), 15
  no creativity, no demo, 18
  practice, 19
  product launches, 12
  startup pitches, 12
  structure, 18
  success, 17

## M, N, O
Memory
  public speaking, 95
  remember your lines
    learn speech by heart, 93
    options, 92
    teleprompter, 94
    trick to hide notes, 93
Mentors, 111

# Index

Metaphor
    creating
        analogy, 29
        similes, 28, 29
    definition, 24
    examples, 24, 25
    practices, 31
    use, 30
    used in technology, 26, 27

## P, Q, R

Passion
    astronomy, 54
    definition, 51
    developers, 52, 53
    devices, 53
    no voice, no passion, 56–58
    practices, 58
    source, 52
    tech arena, coaching speakers, 54, 55

Presentation hacks
    design, 68
    masters, 71, 72
    presentation software, 74, 75
    present slides, 70, 71
    showing code, Kelin Henney, 73, 74

Props
    finding right prop, 65
    inspiration, from other fields, 64
    pitching competition, 62, 63
    practices, 65
    projector, 63

## S

Staging
    definition, 84
    home is a stage, 86, 87
    influence, 87
    prepare yourself, 85
    speaking at cinema, 85
    tech events, 86
    theater stage, Engelbart, 84

Stanford Research Institute (SRI), 15

Story
    crashologist, 8
    first ever tweet, 7, 8
    humanize products, 6
    Internet, 5
    practices, 10
    storytelling, 4
    types, 9

## T, U

Tech stage
    pains techies, 2
    speak in conference, 2
    ten secrets, 2

Teleprompter, 92, 94

## V, W, X, Y, Z

Virtual tech stage
    conference, 97
    conference, benefits, 98
    presentations, 99
    skills
        set own stage, 100, 101
        speak in front of camera, 100
        videoconferencing tools, 99
        virtual world, interaction, 103, 104
        voice, 102

Voxgig's model, 109

GPSR Compliance

The European Union's (EU) General Product Safety Regulation (GPSR) is a set of rules that requires consumer products to be safe and our obligations to ensure this.

If you have any concerns about our products, you can contact us on

ProductSafety@springernature.com

In case Publisher is established outside the EU, the EU authorized representative is:

Springer Nature Customer Service Center GmbH
Europaplatz 3
69115 Heidelberg, Germany

www.ingramcontent.com/pod-product-compliance
Lightning Source LLC
LaVergne TN
LVHW010344260326
834688LV00036B/863